Write-London:
The First Ten Years

Edited by
Naino Masindet and Tom Mallender

Write-London.com

Published in 2025 by Write-London
www.write-london.com

The rights of the individual authors have been asserted under Section 77 of the Copyright, Design and Patents Act 1988 to be identified as the authors of their work.

A CIP catalogue record for this title is available from the British Library
ISBN 9798303920408

All rights reserved. No part of this publication may be reproduced, stored or transmitted in any form or by any means, graphic, electronic, recorded or mechanical, without the prior written permission of a representative of Write-London.

Write-London and the production and printing of this book is supported using public funding by Arts Council England via Grants for the Arts and the National Lottery

Write-London:
The First Ten Years

The work contained in this anthology has been either transcribed from original drafts or compiled from previously published volumes. Any mistakes in the transcription of the work are totally the fault of Tom Mallender and Naino Masindet.

Minor spelling corrections and editorial changes have been made by the editors to some of the work for formatting and space reasons.

Introduction

Write-London has a foundational belief that everyone has a story to tell. We exist to help those stories be heard.

Since 2014, Write-London has been facilitating creative workshops in local communities collaborating with people of all ages and abilities to both express themselves and explore their creativity.

As of December 2024, Write-London has collaborated with over 3,800 participants aged 5-107. This anthology stands as testament to the hard work, effort and the amazing creative vision of those who Write-London has been privileged to work with over the last ten years and look forward to working with for many more years to come.

It is with tremendous pride we present to you this anthology.

Contents

– Poems –

The Ornamentor of Verse	
Tom Mallender	1
Ripple	
Naino Masindet	2
The Canal	
Judi Kennedy	3
There's a Shoe Shop Under My Bed	
Mark Holder	4
1.	
Yaiza Freire-Bernat	5
Hot Air Balloon	
Leslie Aldridge	6
Pathway Closed	
Olivia Jerome	7
Taymouth Castle Library	
Chris Bird	8
Rain	
Zaynab	9
Post-It Note Poems -	
Collectively written	10
Eyes	
Mark Watts	11
Even in Summer, Pavements Are Always Chill	
Chris Bird	12

Fitting Your Life into The Back of a Cab
Carl Gillies   13
Time to Wait
Mark Holder   14
Why?
Asiha Noor   15
Post-It Note Poems
Collectively written   17
Catwalk – A Roundel
Mavis Pilbeam   18
Seasons
Naino Masindet   19
Prose Poem
Diane B   20
My Life in a Children's Home
Leslie Aldridge   21
The Keys Jangle
Suzi Qpid   22
Talking About a Thing
Tom Mallender   24
A Golden Moment
Irene Rabbitts   25
Post-It Note Poems
Collectively written   27
So Long Since We Met
Karen Holden   28
J.E.N.I.F.A
Mark Holder   29

Was a Police Officer
Stacy Nye   30
A Camden Pea-Souper
Julian Penrice   31
Object Poem
Diane B   32
Tik Tok Food
Zaneta Denny   33
Post-It Note Poems
Collectively written   34
Rubble and Air
Mavis Pilbeam   35
Butterflies
Leslie Aldridge   37
His Last Breath
Jackie Poole   38
Redwood
Naino Masindet   39
Gobi Desert, Mongolia
Phoebe Smith   40
Scarves
Mark Holder   41
Before the Angels Came to Mons
Tom Mallender   42
Unrelating Hunger
Chris Bird   44
Declutter Smutter
Suzi Qpid   45

Post-It Note Poems
Collectively written   47
A Conversation between Pen & Paper
Diane B   48
Put That Light Out
Karen Holden   49
Should I Learn to Play the Piano?
Mark Holder   50
The Dust Heap
Angela Bailey   51
PTSD
Leslie Aldridge   52
2.
Yaiza Freire-Bernat   53
She Goes... (A Mind and Memories Lost to Dementia)
Elizabeth Uter   54
Enigma
Chris Bird   55
A Name
Tom Mallender   56
Words Spoken but Never Heard
Phoebe Smith   57
Found Haiku from Chris Bird's Drawing Titles
by Lori Kiefer   58
Stuff That I Like
Mark Holder   59
Structure
Chris Bird   60

– Short Stories –

License to Drive
Webster Forrest   62
Rumi, My Love
Aisha Noor   68
Two Six-Word Stories
Naino Masindet   72
Road to Nowhere
Chris Bird   73
Take My Newt
Webster Forrest   74
The Collector
Elizabeth Uter   79
Two Six-Word Stories
Judi Kennedy   87
Eight Days
Helen Geoghegan   88
The Green Grass of Away
Webster Forrest   91
Two Six-Word Stories
Carl & Stephen   95
Welcome
Chris Bird   96
The Picnic
Hazel Norbury   98
Nan's Front Room
Webster Forrest   105

Therapy
Chris Bird   108
'M3'
Webster Forrest   110

– Write-London Solo Publications –

Human Dilemmas – (All work by Madeleine Kingston)

That Beautiful Town   123
Temporal Lobe Epilepsy   124
Depersonalisation   125
Post Traumatic Stress Disorder   127
The Decision   130

Transmissions – (All work by Chris Bird)

Smoke   145
Hush   146
Slow Motion   147
Street Signs   148
The Walk   149
There I Go   150
Puppet   151
Sanctuary   152

Heroin Will Mislead You	153
The Key	154
They Came from The Shadows	155
Our Side	156

A Medic's Journey to the Falklands –
(Work by Leslie Aldridge) — 158

– Collaborative Projects –

Lost Letters

The Almond Tree
Naino Masindet — 166
The Architecture of Escape
Naino Masindet — 167
Pte Edward George Cutt Two
Chris Bird — 169
Eigengrau
Naino Masindet — 170
Inmates
Tom Mallender — 171
Small Hands
Naino Masindet — 172

Dead Letter
Naino Masindet   173
Being Rowdy Takes a Crowd
Tom Mallender   174
Homesick
Naino Masindet   175
Ten Days Leave
Naino Masindet   176

Poems by Post

A Scandal at School?
Tom Mallender   179
Shining Like Spoken Gold
Chris Bird   180
Walked into Thought
Tom Mallender   181
FEET (The March, 1945)
Mavis Pilbeam   182
Mixed Feelings
Tom Mallender   184
Bell-Song
Mavis Pilbeam   186
Inventive
Tom Mallender   187
Dynasties, Eras and Legacies
Tom Mallender   189

Forgotten
Chris Bird   190
My Part
Tom Mallender   191
Stalag Luft III
Tom Mallender   194

Lost Trades of Islington

Dolly
Tom Mallender   199
Eunice
Tom Mallender   204
Women's Work
Phoebe Smith   205
Why
Phoebe Smith   207
Evacuation
Phoebe Smith   208
Initiation
Phoebe Smith   209
Coach Building
Phoebe Smith   210
Cakes by Post, 1902
Angela Bailey   211
Beale's Store, Holloway: Fraternal Disputes
Angela Bailey   213

– Young Writers –

Let's Write Hammersmith and Fulham 2023

McDonald's
Freeman   215
Adventures in London
Adnan   216
Magic Carpet Story
Rameen   217
Jolof
Voita   218
The Adventure at Pineapple Park
Aya   219
A Fun Time at South Park
Ralph   220
Snippets
Sumaiyah, Intisar   221
The Two Best Friends
Adelaide   222
Another Again
Alisa   223
A Magic Place
Lina   224
Happiness
Angeline   225
The End
Albane   226

Marketplace
Zoya   227
Dragons Are Real
Oscar   228
"What if a koala went on an adventure?"
Cienna, Nadia   229
What is a Griffin?
Sofia   230
Oldilocks
Nadia   231
Mysterious Box – Vegetables
Alessandra   232
"What if you were able to play your sport for your favourite sports team?" Cienna, Linda   233
Light
Albane   234
The Unknown Power
Oscar   235
Lost in a Forest
Henry   236
Love
Albane   237
Short Story
Alessandra   238
The Moon
Zoya   241
Poem
Alessandra   242

The Cave of Mankind's Secrets
Thomas & Nolan   243
Samurai Ninjas
Junaid   245

Sands End Adventures In Creativity

Samurai Ninjas 2
Junaid   248
Bloom Quist
Olivia and Stefy   250
Cat and Dolphin
Maya   252
Untitled
Rosalie   253
Untitled
Nadia   254
Finch
Olivia   255
Welcome to Space
Lina   256
Fortnite
Vivan   257
The Kind Heart
Maya   258
Rocks of Fortune
Rosalie   259

Mrs Meow's Adventure
Lina   260
The Pirate Made of Cheese who Lives in McDonald's
Rosalie   264
KFC
Bonnie and Faith   265
The Girl and The Ghost
Nadia   266
C.A.T Meme Wars
Malia and Max   267
Untitled
Nadia   273
Ukulele Magic
Olivia   274
Don't Do This to Your Heart
Rosalie   275
Spring
Lina   276
Ocean
Olivia   277
Story of the Sad Cloud
Nadia   278
Charlotte and The Chandelier
Olivia   279
Eid and Ramadan
Lina   281
The Meaning of Life
Adelaide   282

Poems

The Ornamentor of Verse by Tom Mallender

The feeling catcher sits
busy unfurling their thought world
distilling with a poorly controlled ink drooler.
Thoughts clear between sound grabbers
become garbled as hand talons
chase them with a word chisel.
The ink drinker fills with self-grown spoils.
The faultless ring-land a poor scribe
making it difficult to gather the word harvest.
Ideas wither, spoil, becoming lost
in the thought world's murk.
What is gathered, trapped or found
is threshed inside the mind mill.
Life's echoes extracted
from shafts sunk deep into self
Thought ores mined, smelted, refined.
Mind forgings worked into ink stains
locked and bound within a thought keeper.
The word smith busy with this sitting work.

Ripple by Naino Masindet

Don't you wonder sometimes about the birds,
The postman,
Where our breath floats to
when it's cold?

Don't you wonder sometimes
about wondering?
Falling into a thought,
refracting the consequence.

The last dying leaf
of the old oak tree.

The Canal by Judi Kennedy

Hidden behind houses
This legacy of a distant industrial past,
Once busy with wharfs and warehouses,
Now abounds with strollers and cyclists.
An odd fisherman sits and ponders.
The bars full of noise and hubbub.

Reflections abound – buildings, trees, graffiti.
This is a new highway for people.

There's a Shoe Shop Under My Bed by Mark Holder

The area under my half of the bed resembles the kind of shoe shop I'd like to visit
You could be transported back in time to the 60's or 70's when you see what's in store

Monkey Boots in black leather with red laces
or in blue or brown suede
Clarks Brogues in black and brown
Oxblood tasselled Penny Loafers
with Dr Martens soles
And camel coloured lace up Hush Puppies.

When I say my HALF of the bed,
in reality it's just a third
Jen has at least twice as many shoes than I have
and much smaller feet.

1. by Yaiza Freire-Bernat

The world is my oyster but my mind's adrift.
I don't know what to do in this world that we live in.

There is so much pain but hope too.
It's like the world can't make up its mind and I can't too.

I know where I want to go, it looks like bliss
Where I have a blank canvas that I get to kiss.

A bit of red here, a bit of blue there
or a touch of green here
in this scape of eternal tints.

Sprawling paints as if they glow, that's what I like,
to let the imagination flow in its chocolate delights.

Bit by bit one step towards humanity
One giant leap for mankind,
Mr Armstrong did it all or was it just his mind.

I guess we'll never know, creativity is a myth
that it's all subjective that even I find amiss.

So ciao my good friend, I will see you anon
in another brain dump or another life along.

Hot Air Balloon by Leslie Aldridge

A trip in a hot air balloon,
This was a journey to capture the countryside soon.
Gliding over the brilliant views,
Over the ocean and sand dunes.
The views glistened in the light,
As the balloon lowered in amongst the trees,
Out of sight.

Pathway Closed by Olivia Jerome

On a winter's day
I went for a walk.
Blue skies
and cotton thickening cloud
were the beauty that my eyes
gazed upon.
The reflection of the sun,
grasped my attention
made me wonder further afield
until I come to a pathway.
To my surprise the pathway
says "Pathway Closed".
Pathway Closed, Pathway Closed.
Stop your time is up.
The beauty of creation
no longer before my eye.

Taymouth Castle Library by Chris Bird

Silent with a carved, wooden heaviness,
The Taymouth Castle library,
Elaborate with oak shadows.

The decorative 1930's space
That looks proud of itself
Depicted on a
Valentines Ltd post card
Strangely subdued, ghostly
And forgotten.

Rain by Zaynab

I love the rain, rain is soft and beautiful,
the best thing for the future.
I like walking in the rain.
I love the sound of the rain,
a nature sound.
The sound of rain in a forest is amazing.
Spring rain is important for nature.

England is a rainy country and I love it!

I like walking in the rain.
In the rain I can think and I can relax.
The landscape light and dreamy.
In the rain I can see wet shadows of trees.

Post-It Note Poems - Collectively written

In its native environment,
the sea dragon is an unequal adversary
for the Paper Mache Tiger

●

Graffiti around a doorway
to nowhere: In Camden
nothing makes sense.

Eyes by Mark Watts

You are
a vertical structure of startled eyes used to
enclose, divide or support a lobeless ear
the bridge of a nose a mouth washed away
by unblinking brickwork

From the block behind you a voice shouts out
"I like music I don't like!" and you can't reply
all you can do is look outwards
towards the infinity that waits in every one of us.

Even in Summer, Pavements Are Always Chill by
Chris Bird

I sat on a folded piece of cardboard;
this was crucial
sleeping in wet trackies is a nightmare.

The slow pattern of commuters began to increase,
dark faces lit by station lights.
Jim had bullied me into it.
He knew what would be taken.
No fooling him by swiping a few quid.

He advised me that 80% of "scrapnel"
came from commuter women,
Muslims the more generous.

My trainers were grey with dirt, so was the
pavement.
Jim always commented,
"London is dirty inside and out, a cruel git."

Fitting Your Life into The Back of a Cab by Carl Gillies

Told by my key worker,
I'm moving that afternoon.
They will get me a cab,
and they're doing me a favour at that.

How do you take a fridge,
a freezer,
a microwave and a new stereo in a cab?

Then you have:
all your clothes,
yourself and the rest of your life
to fit in as well.

That was four years ago.

The stereo is still in its box in my room.
The fridge,
the freezer,
microwave,
and some other stuff I am still waiting for.

I went back but the key worker has moved on.

I really want my microwave.

Time to Wait by Mark Holder

Spent too much time in a bit of a state
I haven't got time to wait

Back with a vengeance and ready to shine
I haven't got time to wait

Long way to go, I'm just sixty one
But I haven't got time to wait

So much to do in this magical world
So I haven't got time to wait

So much to see that my mind's in a whirl
I haven't got time to wait

Full of excitement but I need to stay calm
I need to take time to wait

Must keep my focus and not go too fast
I think I'll take time to wait

Day at a time, simple pleasures to find
61 nowhere near to too late

Why? by Asiha Noor

You were sharing your pain,
your secrets,
in that diary under your bed.

Under the tree, where your swing is still
I read it, now that it's too late.
We used to play under that tree.
You wanted to swing so high,
to touch the clouds.

Higher, Higher, you shouted.
I pushed with all my strength.
Now, you have touched those clouds.

You departed at an inappropriate time.
Sudden.
No farewells.
An abrupt conclusion, with no resolution.

Why this diary?
Why not me?
Why?
Why?

Going back to your room,
I lay the diary where you kept it.
I shall sweep the already well swept room,
change the bed,
draw curtains and switch on the lamp.

Your table is messy.
"Please refrain from tidying my table,
my work gets messed up."
I never listened, not to touch your half-done work.

Would you ever complete this work?
What a question,
life never lets you complete all.

It's raining intensely,
clouds producing shrill cries.
I leave your room.
Never-ending rain,
merges with my everlasting tears.

I think, you never approved of this weather
was that the reason you are gone?

Post-It Note Poems - Collectively written

Alone amongst danger.
Cold paths and winter weather,
lead to deep water.

•

Loving and hating,
two sides of the same penny,
live with the drama.

Catwalk – A Roundel by Mavis Pilbeam

Where'er I walk, I seem to meet some Cat
That sniffs or chats or rolls upon its back,
Tabby or tortoiseshell, ginger or plain black.

The butcher's Cat, of course, is sleek and fat,
But Messy Garden Tabby's flanks are slack –
Where'er I walk, I seem to meet some Cat
That sniffs or chats or rolls upon its back.

Stripes, on the corner, sports a smart cravat,
Bewitching Green Eyes schemes a mean attack,
While Fat Ginge prowls his pavements,
On the track…

Where'er I walk, I seem to meet some Cat
That sniffs or chats or rolls upon its back,
Tabby or tortoiseshell, ginger or plain black.

Seasons by Naino Masindet

Silver summer rays shrill akin to a flashbang
Earthen dreams fall from an entourage of maple
among dancing droplets
Pale winters may still pass
As black stems birth a new shadow
In a lonely stream of forget me nots
And spring...
Spring is a catalytic rebirth
Tropism without consent
A statutory cycle that enables the unfated
to breathe life once more

Prose Poem by Diane B

Travelling forward along your own tapestry. Weaving colours, dropping a stitch or two, losing characters along the way. Adding new patterns which become like friends after a while.

My Life in a Children's Home by Leslie Aldridge

My life started in a children's home,
A three-month-old baby
who couldn't crawl or roam.
As a child without parental support
that would venture life,
To overcome sadness and deal with strife.
Progressing in life with energy and smile
That wouldn't look back for a while,
My path in life was to help in health,
To become a nurse was for myself.

The Keys Jangle by Suzi Qpid

Close…
 …closer
 I can hear keys jangle.
 When will someone open the damn door?

It's not that it's too dark…
that I can't see.
It's that I didn't choose to be here…
It's so damn quiet.
Why am I here?

I can feel my tongue reaching round my teeth.
My mouth is red rust dry
I can hear my brain ticking.
Insistent …trying to make sense of what?
The keys jangle again.
I'm keenly alert…
There's something sharp stabbing my side.
I have deep pockets and wedged in there are the
keys I am hearing.
I pull them out…
Where is the lock?
I can't feel the edges of anything,
even me.

I push forward…
I fall forward…
I tumble, still grasping the keys.
I don't land…
I simply slow down… like clock hands winding backwards.
I can see a small chink in the shadows.
I insert the key….

A light threatens to blind me…

A clinician hands me something plain & flat.
"Here's the report"
I didn't dream it.
Yaay… I'm autistic.
Say hello to your new but not-so-new self.
Free at last
Sarcasm has its own particular innuendo.

Talking About a Thing by Tom Mallender

The thing about dealing with a thing,
or living with the added spice of things,
is that many of us
never really like to talk about the thing or things
as anything other than as a thing.
It's understatement, not willful obscuration.
'tis just a way of dealing with things.

When broached it's often in terms of things,
that things are spoken of as things.

The addition of an adjective or two
gives more meaning or weight to the thing.
A bad thing, a horrible thing,
a grim thing, a really horrible thing.
A thing for everything.

It's good practice to talk about things
when you can leave them as things.

A Golden Moment by Irene Rabbitts

I was taught to love every living thing
Plant, animal and fish, mum succeeded well
I especially took to creepy crawlies
With no fear, but respect and to be careful

We had the usual pets over time
Cats, dog, stray budgie,
guinea pigs, my sister's ducks
When there were too many mice at school
They inevitably came home – to stay

I was the child who kept caterpillars
Researched their food, looked to their care
Finding out what they needed and when
Taking joy when they metamorphosed into
beautiful moths

Frogs were not popular with mum
And had to stay in the pond, or at least outdoors
But the one thing I wasn't allowed to acquire
Was a snake, on sale in the local pet shop

Pocket money was saved, tank prepared
Research completed already
But for once no persuasion worked on mum

And no snake was to come home, period!

I only learned later how scared she was
And I never found out why, to this day
The years went by and I never did keep snakes
Then sadly mum got dementia

But one day in the care home we joined her
For the latest special activity – 'exotic pets'
And there was my mum with an enormous snake
She'd forgotten her fears and was holding it up
Wearing the biggest smile you could ever wish for

Dementia is terrible and took her away
She died a few years ago now
But I'll never forget seeing my mum and the snake
Her fears all gone, she was free
For one beautiful golden moment in all that sadness
There's my mum, and the snake, and a dirty great smile
Such a wonderful memory for me

*We met Irene at the Laureate's Lounge Open Mic Night in Staines, where Write-London was performing, when she debuted this poem and asked her if we could include it in this collection

Post-It Note Poems - Collectively written

The same roads.
Some vanished places, names sticking.
The brook there, still a brook.

●

Found in a variety of classics.
Are secret
gardens.

So Long Since We Met by Karen Holden

I will never forget.
The harmonica shop,
and the nail-salon with a claw-like hand
in its window.
Walking along Hendon High Street.
I also recall, gathering anticipation
of our meeting in your tiny room!
I step past the red phone-box
and the pavement repair shaped like Africa,
outside your door.

J.E.N.I.F.A by Mark Holder

She's got blonde hair
She wears cool clothes
She loves cats and Wham
She really hates to pose

She's got great taste
She likes procedural drama
She doesn't eat meat
She hates Bananarama

She puts up with me
She misses her brother
She's the best thing in my world
Man, I don't half love 'er

Was a Police Officer by Stacy Nye

A chase.
Quinn.
Outside number 39.
Blackledge.
The suspect was Liam Quinn.
Blackledge noticed.
Shot Tibble twice.
A 38 long.
Tibble died.
Was married.

A Camden Pea-Souper by Julian Penrice

Born in a London smog,
the year of the coronation.
Jack the Ripper utilised the smog to his benefit.
Doubtful,
that the smog was from diesel buses,
during his reign from Hell.

Medical researchers have tested my lungs
to see the effects of smog upon them.
Can't see your way ahead, need a torch.
Unless there is a blackout,
then you will be fined.

The Clean Air Act really has stood up.
Police used to still be out in the pea-soupers.

It's different today
I still can't see very far ahead,
but today that's me.

Object Poem by Diane B

Mouse with no tail
Mouse with no house
Mouse with no eyes
Mouse that points and opens up pages to view
Mouse that clicks
Mouse mouse if only you knew

Tik Tok Food by Zaneta Denny

You've seen it on socials,
You've been pretty vocal
Boredom drives you to visit
You just have to experience it.

That coffee shop, burger joint,
Apparently the taste is on point, say reviewers
That chicken skewer, delicious
You watch them as they eat.
Will you fulfil the same feat?
Alight in central London and scurry down a side street.

You grumble and frown at the queue.
You don't behave, it's true.
You get your food, everyone acting like it's a zoo.
Finally you're part of the club now, with your find, uou're through.

Post-It Note Poems - Collectively written

Danger-
No Illegal swimming.
No Legal swimming.
Swimmers will be asked to leave.

Rubble and Air by Mavis Pilbeam

When I get home
my house has gone,
my half of the pair
just rubble and air.
Next door's stands tall,
detached, vertical.
I look about in despair;
mine's not there.

Been a bad night,
fright after fright
driving that thing,
bells clanging.
Just want home
but no, it's gone.
Stand and stare -
it's just not there.

Cuppa next door:
"We lay on the floor
under the grand pianer,
felt the blast hammer,
pianer strings twanging -
Heaven's bells clanging?"
"I'm off home," but where?

Home's not there.

They come in helmets,
salvage a few bits:
mother's best table.

Butterflies by Leslie Aldridge

My interest in butterflies
was imaginative as a child,
I would search the garden through the wild.

The Red Admiral was beautiful in manner,
To captivate the species was glamour.

Butterflies gliding through the air,
would land on flowers in the summer glare.

The tortoiseshell with its amazing bright colours,
Surrounded by the bright flowers.

His Last Breath by Jackie Poole

The rhythm of that dance: galloping horses,
jumping fences, in a race.
Black horses in a white hospital room,
keeping up the pace,
You were just a breath, your body a balloon,
hollow breath, delayed death.
Waxed masked, gurning garish
ghoul, departure delayed till mourn.

Redwood by Naino Masindet

Beneath the fallow hills and barren trees
I am a seed
Waiting for a long expired spring
Tears silenced by rain
Quiet as my fleeting memory
I was never the redwood I'd dreamed of becoming.

Gobi Desert, Mongolia by Phoebe Smith

Yes has become my default,
drinking fermented mare's milk,
eating something beige,
a swiss roll relayed from the nearest town
a hundred kilometres away.
A celebration, a surprise, my birthday.
      Yes has become my default,
      drunk on milk and fermented swiss roll
      I ride the gobi like a bandit queen,
      undeterred and undaunted
      by my total inexperience,
      the children's hysterical laughter
      a confirmation.
      Yes has become my default.

Scarves by Mark Holder

I've got one in paisley
A red one with white dots
One in plain burgundy
And a green one with cream spots

A pink one with black diamonds
A nice black and gold one too
A green one with a red motif
By the way, the paisley one's blue

They're mostly made by Tootal
A timeless, classic label
Jen, she buys me most of 'em
They make me feel like I'm Clark Gable

Before the Angels Came to Mons by Tom Mallender

Jay Naylor watched and listened.
A boy in the BEF,
3rd division's trumpeter.

An indeterminate grey mass,
slowly approaching.

"Four hundred,
three fifty,
at three hundred."
The officer was saying.

A grey wall no longer.
Individual details,
starting to stand out.

It was made of men.
Starting to get rather anxious,
frightened even.

The officer sounded still
still as cool as anything,
At two fifty,
at two hundred."

Then.

"Ten rounds rapid!"
The chaps opened up.
As a boy of 16 I was astounded.
Will never forget.

Unrelenting Hunger by Chris Bird

Antipsychotic medication
bloats the human shape
in a distinct and irreversible manner.
Plump faces and swollen bellies
commonplace in wards and day centres,
-zapine's leading to overeating.

Declutter Smutter by Suzi Qpid

Moving stuff,
Huffing, puffing,
Shifting, lifting…
Clearing space.

Liberating floors…
Discarding… Decluttering
Smutter in my head,
Do I need it.
Toss it aside instead.

Wheezing, sneezing,
Must dust more often.
All those forgotten places
All those familiar faces
In photos challenge me afresh
Do I like these things… nah
Do I love that 80s bling?

My aching back chimes
How about that new bed
stuck in its box.
Time to slice and dice the plastic
New bouncy comfort unlocked
In a whirling frenzy of mad energy

I feel bloody fantastic
Even though it's giving off gasses
Smells worse than a stinky welly

Throw those curtains wide
Let me swish and glide
Towards the windows.
A few puffs on my asthma inhaler
Out damn stuffy stale everything
Now I've earned a massive long snooze.

Post-It Note Poems - Collectively written

A damp graveyard
complete with stereotypical
black cat.

•

Healthy gargoyles
enjoy
staring.

A Conversation between Pen & Paper by Diane B

"Hey, use me."
"Hey, why don't you pick me?"
"It's no use, they don't need us anymore."
"I dream of a power failure."
"Oh me too."
"They used to pick us up to carry us around just in case they needed us. Now…?"
"I know, no one asks to borrow me anymore…"
"'Save the trees! Save the trees!' That is the big cry…"
"Recycle, reuse."

Put That Light Out by Karen Holden

Born 1939,
Into the dark
Keeping people safe
But how?
No lit cigarettes
Tripping over paving stones
Cobbles noisy underfoot
Mothers grasping trembling hands
"Stay close, don't let go!"
Planes overhead
What does it mean
Sirens screeching,
Running, hiding.
All clear sounds safe for now
But still the blackout.
Born again 1945.

Should I Learn to Play the Piano? by Mark Holder

What does the right hand do
                            that the left doesn't do?
A chord's a chord whatever instrument you use
I'm sure that I could master it if I should so choose
Yes I think I'll learn to play the pianner

The Dust Heap by Angela Bailey

1902
Covent Garden at its peak.
Young women and girls,
beautiful and elegant,
searching among the debris
seeking a living at the tip.

It truly was their living,
bits of leftovers and whatever they find.

Sifting for objects,
even though they were not worth keeping,
to keep them alive.

Survival the only expectation,
bent over backwards,
scrambling for "treasures".

Old cloths, scraps of rags,
ashes clean and not so,
oyster shells, bits of tin and perhaps salvageable
paper and un-burnt coal
with the hope of a pearl or lost golden ring.

"Treasures",
the alternative to ruin or death.

PTSD by Leslie Aldridge

Post Trauma is a shock reaction
from an incident that leaves
the mind with a lasting memory
for some time.

Trauma is the initial event that
gives the brain an initial reaction
of flashbacks, like an
explosion of a landmine.

Stress symptoms can develop
like anxiety, tremors and nightmares
all having a lasting effect.

Disorder is the result of the trauma
and shock to the brain.
this can be helped by counselling
and treatment that can be met.

2. by Yaiza Freire-Bernat

A heart in pieces,
what do you do?

When your life's been turned upside down
and you realise you're through.

One step at a time, that's all it takes,
to mend the broken pieces that have gone astray.

A bit of silver! Oh that's what I'll do!
To create a silver lining that's still connected to you.

I'm still missing pieces but I think I'll be okay,
because I know that dawn still leads
to another day.

She Goes…
(A Mind and Memories Lost to Dementia)
by Elizabeth Uter

 When no one was looking
    she opened all the doors
  and let them in.
    One by one they crept by
thin as the midday shadows
  lining the walls,
              No words dropped from
their bloodless lips
       No sound colliding
  with the polished floors.
       Only the smell
    of bitter tears
the fleeting taste
    of irony in the air.
Past regrets,
   broken dreams,
              unrequited memories,
                       drifting
beyond
  the unravelling halls

       and vanishing through small
windows.

Enigma by Chris Bird

Cryptic links connect
objectively unrelated words
in an unsettling pattern:

Telephone, Elephant.

These nouns
signifying separate formal meanings
are linked when I see them.

Hospital contains the malign word *pit*.
Medicine encompasses the negative term *sin*.
Holborn responds to the concept *burn*.

Lion. Liar. Zion.
Treat. Trick. Tie.
Con. Crown. Can of Cola.
Tan. Tarantula. Taint.

A Name by Tom Mallender

I was born on Thor's day,
during a thunderstorm.
Fitting that Mjölnir rang upon the anvil
as the son to a smith was born.

The latest Mallender.
A maker of hammers in rough translation.

Tradition broke with me,
first for generations not
Richardbjorn Richardson.

Thomas Richard, was I christened.
Named after my father's tutelary.

For centuries the name Mallender
has not moved beyond
the Parish of St Josephs.
Limestone epitaphs stand there.
Smiths and builders, craftsmen, farmers
horsemen all
every first-born son
Richard son of Richard.

That all changed when I was born on a Thursday.

Words Spoken but Never Heard by Phoebe Smith

You were never one of my favorites.
It was difficult to warm you,
always so angry and mean and resentful.
I always hoped that given time
you'd grow out of it,
but that's never going to happen now.
All the neighbors have been very kind,
very generous.

Your local reputation has certainly changed,
nobody calls you a bloody nuisance anymore
now you've become a brave, brave boy…
And like millions of mothers with dead sons
we are told that we should be brave,
yet the 'bravery' implies a situation with choices,
the possibility of alternatives.

I refuse to be brave,
I want to slam doors in frustration and spite.
I want to smash windows and hear breaking glass.
I want to turn on all the taps and watch sinks overflow.
I want to swear and curse with words I can't pronounce.

I want you to know you were never my favorite,
I want you to know that I'm sorry.

Found Haiku from Chris Bird's Drawing Titles
by Lori Kiefer

Halloween rave
papier mache stars dissolve -
like the night.

Stuff That I Like by Mark Holder

West side of London for rivers and parks
Then travel North for thrills after dark
All of the time that I spend with my Jen
Or pubs, gigs and clubs with my circle of friends

Beer, wine or whisky while I'm listening to soul
With a shed load of crisps sat in a bowl
A new pair of brogues fit snug to my feet
While I'm throwing some shapes
to a Disco Funk beat

Laying in bed on a dank Saturday
With a tea and toast from a plate on a tray
Short trips to Lisbon, Madrid or to Barca
These are the joys that I'm forever after

Structure by Chris Bird

Tea and coffee are a light bulb
to the moths of mental illness.

Tea bags and tablespoons of instant coffee
pinned the empty hours to the structure of the day.

Short Stories

License to Drive by Webster Forrest

"That must be so amazing."

"A driving license?"

"When I get mine, I'm going on a long, long road trip right across the States. I'll start in Vermont and go all the way down to Key West."

"I did that."

"Really? Oh my God that's my dream."

"Well we went from Key West to Buffalo - not Vermont."

"Buffalo. Not as sexy as Vermont, but I'd take it."

"I enjoyed it. It was beautiful watching the scenery change so dramatically along the route."

"I can imagine."

"I mean - you start in Key West, so you go from storm-battered old houses with sagging verandas to that absolutely crazy raised highway that stretches out over the open water for miles and miles so you can't even see the end of it."

"Oh yeah! I love that. I can't wait to drive along that."

"And then you hit Miami which looks like a spaceship crash-landed on a beach. Then you just follow the coastal up into Georgia where the road looks like a runway banked by millions of pine trees.
Savannah is just about the prettiest place I've ever been. All the old historical houses and the faded grandeur of boulevards lined with live oaks bending into the gap. The Spanish moss suspended from every crooked bough, gracefully caressed by a hot breeze. It's intoxicating."

"What was your favourite part of the journey?"

I had to think for a moment.

"I'm going to say rural Pennsylvania."

"Pennsylvania? Sounds boring."

"It's mysterious. Those quiet old Pennsylvania farm houses couched amid dark rolling lawns shrouded in mist. It's incredibly atmospheric; there's something very reserved about it. Everything looks tidy and well-tended. Anyway.
What about you?
This is your story. What would you want to see?"

"For me it's more about the freedom. Just being on the open road with no barriers, free to go wherever I want. I might just wing it and drive around aimlessly."

"Really? I thought you wanted a specific route."

"I don't really know what I want. All I know is that I want to be able to sit in a car, close the door, lock the car, turn on the engine, put it in gear and then just go. Just go and go and go and go."

She looked down at the pen she'd been playing with for the past few minutes.

"Anything to get away from here."

"What's wrong with here?"

She chucked the pen on to the table, sat back, and ran her hands through her long hair and looked away to one side. I could see there were tears in her eyes. Finally, she turned and looked at me.

"Nothing is ever about me."

"What do you mean?"

"Well take this story for example - this is just a writing exercise, but it was supposed to be from my perspective, but it's not been. It's all been about what you have done. Not about me."

"It seems to be about you now."

"Yeah, well that's only because I started crying."

I scrunched up my mouth and gave her a sympathetic frown. She was so young. How could she know what it was really like to be free, since she wasn't yet independent of her parents?

"I just want my freedom."

"Freedom comes with responsibilities."

"I know. I know that. I do. It's just - I haven't really experienced freedom yet, so I'm - I guess I'm just nervous. And eager to have it. Freedom."

"When's your driving test?"

"Tomorrow."

"Do they issue the license right away?"

"Yup. On the spot: like a temporary one - but it's a full license. You get a card one later in the mail."

"So today could be your very last day of not having freedom."

The light in her eyes lifted up, and her lips parted into a little grin.

"Sounds like something to celebrate."

She quickly held up one hand and shook her head.

"I don't want to jinx my test tomorrow."

"I don't believe in jinxing. It's a cop out. If you believe in yourself, then you won't worry about jinxing things."

She put her arms around me and gave me a hug.

"Come on. Let's go for pizza. My treat. Hey - do you have your provisional license with you?"

She nodded with a tearful smile.

I chucked her the keys.

Rumi, My Love by Aisha Noor

It was a cold winter evening in Konya. Darkness had not yet descended but people were busy feeding more oil into the streetlamps before lifting them up to light the curvy streets.

At the end of the street was a Maikhana (house of alcohol) where noble society was never seen. When they visited, they were masked behind big woollen shawls. Drunkards and other outcasts don't care, they were loud, whistling and singing.

Like most nights, the streets around the Maikhana became busier as the darkness thickened.

This evening, the street is crowded with well-dressed, well-mannered educated young boys from well-known families. There are so many of them blocking the way, preventing prostitutes with cheap bold make up and their clients from passing through.

Policemen, alert with their hands on the swords, are ready to deal with any unlawful encounter. A few prostitutes are inquiring why they cannot get through but receive no prompt answers from the police.

Suddenly a dervish, Shamas - a slim, tall man with long curly hair in his early forties wearing an old juba - stops by the crowd and jumps off his donkey. One of the women takes hold of its reins and kisses the donkey's forehead who shows his love by waving his tail.

"Salaam girls, what is going on?" Says Shamas. "Ruksan, why are you all standing here?" He asks one of the young men in the crowd.

"Shamsu, they're warning us about the Maikhana. Don't know why, but they think…" Rukhsan says pale and wide-eyed.

One of the many students approached from the crowd laughing. "I know you. You are a black magician, you came to our madrasa while Maulana Rum was teaching us."

Shamas smiles a smile sweet as honey, his voice very soft. "Oh, so you are one of Maulana's students. Son, I am not a practitioner of Black magic; I am a practitioner of love."

The student refuses to shake hands. A few more students join them. Another boy shouts, "You are a magician! You threw our books and Maulana's scripts into the pond! When he asked you who you were, you never responded but threw all the books!"

Shamas says he recalls the incident, but adds that he never damaged their books. He recovered them as dry as before.

"That was magic! How did the books stay dry?" Shouted one of the boys.

Shamas was calm, smiling.

The students shouted, calling him names. One said, "because of your mysterious act, our Maulana became under you spell. A man of great Islamic Hadith and philosophy stopped teaching us."

Another shouted, "Our Maulana is behaving so out of character. He is singing and dancing, whirling along like a drunkard, and today we came to know he is meeting you at the Maikhana, is it true?"

Shamas again smiled. "We are both searching for eternal love, only one ray of that love has brought us to this stage. The love of Allah, when it enters your heart, you love all his creations."

A student wanted to know more. Curious, he asked, "Dervish, but we are Muslims. We are told not to mingle with prostitutes or visit Maikhana?"

Shamas answered, "We are told not to drink or enter zina, but simultaneously we are instructed to distribute our love unconditionally. So now please let these ladies go to work. That is their means of living, they have hungry kids and cold cottages which needs food and fire."

The students let the women though.

Shamas followed sitting on his donkey singing a melodious tune in Persian, *"Together in his company, we cross the occasion of love. We are swimming and drowning but haven't found the deepest surface yet."*

Two Six-Word Stories by Naino Masindet

Photographer slips over, only snaps neck.

Reality: a sandbox of sentient stardust.

Road to Nowhere by Chris Bird

Near the station there was always a collection of junkies and homeless people, more of whom seemed to appear at dusk. As the working day descended into shadow, the Gothic towers only added to the gloom as traffic remained relentless. Neon lights shone in gaudy colour above people waiting, cigarette smoke trailing. I embraced their degeneration and self-loathing.

I never envied the suited and booted, the mortgage dependent, the rent slaves; all constrained and defined by work. Their footsteps hit the grey pavements as they rush from office computers or congested sandwich bars. The sense of exclusion is double edged.

Sitting in an alcove watching the Victorian station could seem the most wonderful experience after using. Traffic noises and passing trickles of chatter provide a fleeting background. People walk by usually discussing TV, food, shopping or sports, sometimes a snatch of politics.

In the distance, a police siren showed London was still alive. The yearning to score was already rising inside me but bearable for now. Tomorrow?

Take My Newt by Webster Forrest

Some things just seem larger than they are. Less often, they feel smaller than they are. Lemme give you a forinstance - that's what my friend Larry used to say, 'a forinstance', as though it were one word. (You and I know better.) Anyway, here's my 'forinstance'.

When I was a little boy in short trousers, scrambling around in the back garden playing with my toys and digging holes, I happened to find a newt living in our small pond. Being a boy of a certain age and disposition, I was naturally the owner of a small fishing net. So I went to the garage and got my net. And caught the newt.

I didn't have anywhere to keep a newt, so I had to construct a little home for him out of available things I was able to find in the garage. On this occasion that amounted to a gallon jar, with lid, a few pieces of gravel from when my dad was digging a path in the garden, and a stick I found outside and broke in half so it would fit inside the jar. I washed the gravel, or pebbles, or whatever they were, put that in the jar, then washed the stick, dropped that in, and then filled the jar up with rainwater from the barrel under the down-pipe from the roof. I was pretty proud of myself, because it looked really good. Then, in went the newt.

At first, he just floated there a couple of inches from the bottom totally motionless and with his little arms and legs stretched out, but then after a while, he suddenly twitched and came back to life and started swimming around with his mouth up against the glass looking for a way out.

Now, I'm no idiot - I know you gotta give animals air. Air, water, and food. Obviously water was covered, but I had to make sure it could breathe, and at the same time, I had to make sure it could not escape. So I took a nail and a hammer and made a load of holes in the lid of the jar - and before you ask, I hammered the holes from the inside upwards, so that the spiky edges would not be facing towards the freedom-obsessed amphibian, lest he somehow get up there and scrape his face off.

Now there was just the question of food. I went to our home encyclopedia and found that newts spend almost all of their time in water, and that they eat worms and grubs and insects and even small fish or anything that they can fit into their small but conspicuously wide mouths.

I went out into the garden. There weren't any particularly obvious worms, grubs, or insects out and about in the garden, so I ventured down into the ravine and started looking around under rocks for beetles and centipedes and worms and things. I had a mason jar with me and collected them into it. By the end of my scavenging trip, I had quite a little collection of creepy-crawlies for Mr. Newt, so I returned to the family home. This is where things turn south.

I ran back up to the house. The back door was locked, which is something I had not done. I went round to the side door, which goes into the kitchen. It, too, was locked. Finally, I came to the front door. Locked. Mother must have gone out to do some shopping and, well, I was going to say, "thinking I must be upstairs...", but she can't have even called out, because if she had, there would have been no reply, and she would have gone to investigate and found that I was nowhere to be found, and on this basis would - or should - have gone looking for me and not simply got into her car and left.

Fortunately, I remembered that I had left a basement window unlocked the last time I was poking around in the window well (they often contained toads, doomed to death or salvation by me) so fortunately I was able to get back inside. I went up into the kitchen. I was alone in the house. I put my jar of insects on the kitchen counter and looked in the fridge. It contained a pie. Well, should my mother be flattened by an eighteen-wheeler on the freeway, I would at least not starve.

There wasn't anything in the fridge. I mean, it was full of food, but none of it jumped out at me and made me want to eat it. I couldn't believe my mother would actually just get up and leave me alone in the house. Or maybe this was a test! I immediately dismissed the test idea. It was too risky and the unexpectedness of it was not my mother's style. No, it was far more likely that she had been abducted by aliens or that a former lover came here and abducted her.

I looked over at the jar of bugs. Some of them were starting to eat each other. I decided if I didn't feed them to my newt fast, there would just be one big fat bug left. The one who had eaten all the others. I took my jar into the mud room where the newt was. There was the jar, the water with the stick floating in it, and the rocks at the bottom. But there was no newt. The lid was off and there was no newt.

A while later, after watching some TV and making myself a sandwich and coming to the conclusion that my mother had indeed left me to die, I had occasion to use the bathroom. Who should I see staring up at me inside the toilet bowl but Mr. Newt? Having forsaken the home which I had lovingly created especially for him, he had evidently by some natural instinct found his way to the nearest body of water available: the toilet.

I thought of my mother and I thought of the day. I came to the conclusion that nobody in my family was fit for parenthood, least of all myself, and so, with a surprising lack of remorse, I flushed the newt away. Spin, spin little green friend, perhaps I shall be ready one day.

The Collector by Elizabeth Uter

Spy cameras hang from shadowy buildings, like fleas sucking on a dog's back. They monitor the visit of 26th century collector, Benton C. His medic-wristwatch, the Dr. Paracelsus model – Dr P, for short – with female voice, breathes into his senses, "…Please, Benton C, vacate. You have reached Cheapside, late 21st century, the City of London…"

This is the first known footage of Benton C as he travels on a cloud of deep and painful thought. Inverting reality as he goes at great personal cost to himself, to be here, 500 years in his past with a diminishing window of thirty minutes to "declutter" in a manner that is within acceptable work parameters, then catch his ride home.

He sucks in the fetid air and hawks it straight out. Filthy-dirty air, cold. Never imagined it like this. But really, what else to expect from Neanderthals? He looks his surroundings up and down, like a prissy drill sergeant inspecting sleazy troops. His lips veer downwards at the drab, stinking mess of the street. Where's their sense of hygiene? How can they live like this? An obvious reflection on their degenerate souls. Many of the well-thumbed books

– a million to be exact – he's memorised, he's mind-hacked to mental memory chip – a million to be exact – to support this view; Benton C refuses to dwell on the googolplexian celebrated tomes that state otherwise.

So, this is where the rot sets in. His arsenic-grey eyes click to and fro, focusing on the living auras as they cling like 'hell ants' to the besieged quarters, which in turn, tilt towards him like a badly earthed, 'electric joy-coast ride. Bouncing sonar bubbles of H_2S gas drift towards him. His eyes water, his nose prickles and his nails snag and scratch at itchy fingers encased within plasti-clad gloved mittens.

He is momentarily caught in the flickering lens of a concealed window cam, an unflattering snapshot, forever staggering in a drunk-about-to-fall walk, possibly a ruse, for he certainly appears sober in all other respects. He leans slightly into his walk as the elderly sometimes do or a puppet stopping and slanting in its tracks. First his knee, then his whole leg aching in a crazy spasm, lifting high as if lunging over hurdles at a slow man's Olympics causing his booted feet to slide in the sludge of the pavement where the bones of small, dead animals break with an aching screech under the crunch of his precarious, relentless tread, releasing a newborn stench akin to a thousand sweaty gym shoes smothered in rotting cheese. He opens his mouth dismayed and wishes he hadn't, for now he tastes its rancid discharge, it coats his tongue and every breath he takes.

On this narrow walkway, his body brushes against the walls of a gated environ and his touch triggers corrupting blooms that puff and drizzle mould onto his non-standard protective gear, which seemed a good choice at the start of his journey. He is bundled into 1970's culture-appropriated magma-cooled grey suit, shiny shirt, black bowler hat drip-moulding to his head like fresh-trimmed hair, He's a hapless Mr. Ben lookalike, in at the deep end, crusading in this forbidden arena of life and death.

His skin is gently petted by the rolling face of his graphene-studded medi-watch, the countdown's afoot.
Dr. P coos, "…Please, Benton C, precisely 20 minutes to go…" He turns and there is a bittersweet-orange street sweeper's cart. He peers in, out, quick as a spitting cobra, reeling from the fishy, maggoty steam gushing from its depths. A

tiny 'voice ad' whispers in his head. *"There are consequences, you know? What if you're not really here, Benton C? If you are really all alone and this is just a simi-vision? We, at Century News Corps 26, aim to provide hyperarousal-hallucinations to suit your every need. Or maybe you require an out-of-the-soul-induced dream?"* A muscle ticks in his jaw. Concerned, Dr. P kicks in, administering 2000mg of Rescue Salve to mute the ever present, low level, glitchy tabloid noise. Benton C straightens his back. *No, no, I am definitely here.*

He squeezes a gloved finger and thumb into his jacket pocket and plucks out a drab, three inch electronic device and an All-Purpose O. Wilde stylus, which drawls, like the playwright, at intervals, "True pens stab to the paper's heart, Bosie." Benton C gloats. *I am face front interacting with redundant life forms… like this cart, ha-ha-ha!* His eyes disappear into a rigid gurn. He kicks his heavily booted foot at what he thinks is a rock which is in his way, a hideous yelp and a greasy smear underneath his boot alerts him that he's caught the tail and a back leg of a neon-glowing, mange-ridden, pygmy fox. He lifts his boot and it limps away to a hidey-hole in the ground. He watches with forensic interest and follows behind, his superior nostrils flaring as he bends to examine the area. Dr. P caresses, "Please, Benton C, your collection is nearly complete. 10 minutes and counting."

Slime drips from the nearest building and smacks the side of his head, trickling down to his shoulder; he swivels to look up then jerks his body away from the offending corner, his smile fading. *Up to my nose in crap. I want a desk job and no more fieldwork.* He closes his eyes. *I'm better than this.* He breathes gently in, out. The medi-watch intones, "Empty disharmonious thoughts." As the tiny handheld screen device in his hand fizzes and flickers into life, his eyes snap open. A purchase order pops up and he's forced to ignore the putrefying mess on his clothes. He quickly ticks and crosses relevant boxes on his job lot and, with his cranky stylus, attempts to write a brief report, headed '21st Century Losses'. He gouges at the page surface again and again with the pen tip until reluctant trickles of fluid sputter out, slowly permeating the screen to form the appropriate phrases.

He taps the device once; it expands a hand's breadth and a myriad of lights flicker the length.

He scans the dustbin cart, a green light halos it. Whirring clicks sound and a photoflash slides out to record the cart. Taps twice and a red light erupts. He clears his throat. Always the dross, the rubbish, never a drop of elixir in sight.

Unnoticed, a glove peels from his hand, Dr. P issues a red, throbbing warning light. He scratches his nose. Hmmm.... item emits sufficient electromagnetic waves. He slaps the device; it folds into itself and he shoves it back in pocket. Dr. P shrieks, "Toxic tissue alert!" His ungloved hand is shrivelling and turning blue. Two pin-sized rollers extend from Dr. P and bite into his dying flesh, diffusing a cure-all solution. The colour returns, *lucky-lucky*, he chirps as the skin plumps.

"5 minutes to clear area," Dr. P's warning blues blare out. Benton C squints at the medi-watch. *Just a few more items and I'm off.*

Both of his eyes stretch and split to look for locals but freeze when a car light glares in his face. Glass from his protective goggles splinters and dusts his jacket. Dr. P screams, "Lens failure!" Benton C sets off fast but leans too far into his walk, it stalls him. His knee creaks and bleeds. Bad! He shifts his other leg, it seizes up, judders, gives way, falling with a crack. He struggles on the pavement. Discount suit melting. *Should've paid extra for neutron-star pure protective gear.* Cheapness. Low standards. Cutting corners. Instant gratification. He coughs guiltily. *Now what?* he grumps but stops when two heavies in dark-suited leather stride up, stopping beside him. Waiting to cross the glowing, snarled up road. Benton C completes a mind smirk and angles dutifully towards them like a pen scratching a notepad. One crows, "Bikers're the new city boys, yeah?" The other flexes tattooed knuckles. Benton arches them a less than secret look. *Really?*

He slips the O. Wilde stylus from his pocket, tilts in towards the men and with it, tap-guides and fells them both - they fall deep and sleeping in the cart. Almost clear. Gripping the handlebars, Benton C crosses the road, his suit in tatters, malfunctioning as he goes. Buildings, pavements, streetlights whirl and suck into the cart, along with oncoming cars from the smoky waste of the rush hour. Everything, disappearing into the machine.

"One minute to clear area," The metallic soul of his medi-watch shrills and one last time, that ice smile to camera. "History recorded and erased."

And now, in deep and painful thought once more, he turns away and isn't three-dimensional at all but like a cartoon character bulldozed flat and walking upright, somehow slipping sideways and in that hesitant, sidewise walk, flickering in and out of vision. He's cleaning up the ages, merging into future hours, having rewritten the messy past, the conqueror of all time. He reaches for the clouds.

Two Six-Word Stories by Judi Kennedy

Kraken wakes. Ocean shakes. Sailor quakes.

Hammer. Fled. Vermilion head. Enemy dead.

Eight Days by Helen Geoghegan

Monday: The three ladies in the ward were waiting when I came; they had been waiting all day. I came to see the fourth lady, the loud one who got the most visitors.

Tuesday: When I was at the dentist, I thought about the old ladies waiting. I wanted to go back. I wanted to see what I could see in the waiting room. They looked like they were rehearsing something silently while they were being ignored. The amount of time they spent waiting was about the same amount of time they were ignored. I didn't work that out with my head.

Wednesday: The dentist knew a lot about the bone in my jaw. I am definitely excited about one of the ladies; she has confirmed that there are better tracks of information than the one from my head. Good news - my head is swollen, tired.

Thursday: I woke thinking about Annette, one of the ladies. It's been a while since I woke with someone's name on my lips. I feel her presence play near my heart. I didn't know that this kind of infatuation was available.

Friday: My mind keeps feeding my heart information about Annette; I have no way of checking if it is true. So what!

Saturday: I wanted to give a small gift to one of the ladies but the one across from her is already jealous that my eyes go straight to her. Jealousy is uncomfortable when you are mobile and romance is involved; it must be even more uncomfortable if you are confined to a bed and the one getting attention wears two odd shoes. The lady I was visiting asked me why I kept 'looking over there.' A bit harassed from having my attentions blocked I became bold. I just walked over and placed the cream on her locker.

Sunday: When I got there, she was sitting in one of the two chairs across from the nurse's station. "It was you," she said. I was pleased about her tracing equipment. Little fountains of bubbles, in me.

Monday: No one waiting for attention today. The ladies were all between limbo and longing. The heat of the ward was warming the three smells, which were impossible to name or get comfortable in. There was music playing from a blue plastic machine. It seemed a little too loud, insistent for

'You belong to me'. I sat there watching the ladies drift. The song was hurting me. I tried to reason with myself. Not much luck. I had been a good visitor until then. The next song was 'I'll be seeing you in all the old familiar places.' I told myself I shouldn't have come. It was a dangerous kind of socialising, prey to smells, old love songs and ladies in nightdresses. Mine was the only heart not in a bed, the wrench in the smothered cry told me it was keening. I should take it somewhere else. I wanted to go but I couldn't move.

They were sleeping to get away from the ward and each other. And I was there, touching.

The Green Grass of Away by Webster Forest

"Oh that engine! I still got it ringing in my ears." She leapt up out of the old blue Lincoln like a scalded cat. She raised her arms over her head and then spread her elbows and ran her hands through her hair.

"Oh, feel that air! Did you ever have such a feeling as pure fresh country air after a long car ride. I forgot what clean air smelled like."

She'd already put a distance of about a hundred feet between herself and the dusty overheated 'land barge', as she called it. It was cooling down and the engine was ticking as various metal shrouds and housings and shafts and bolts all began slowly to contract back to their original size.

The first order of business was going to be seeing to the house, but they were both so wrecked by the journey that they yielded to the grass's beckon call. Neither of them spoke for several minutes.

The unpleasant cloud that had lingered over their day since the argument in the motel was still there but it was fighting a losing battle for predominance over the future hours. Its combatant was the sense of relief, gratitude, and just calm that they both felt on getting out of the city.

"Listen," Amanda said, wishing to knock it on the head right away, before they even went through the front door.

"We don't have to." said Loren, holding his hand up. He hadn't said a word for at least seventy miles, and the one word he did say before that was cows, when they had driven through a field of them.

"What do you mean we don't have to?"

"Have the argument. The one that's in each of us: pre-programmed. We can just walk away from it, and let it go. Just like we eventually would if we took the argument route."

"You mean like, 'the bridge is out, take this road instead and get there all the same'?"

"Yes. I just think it's time we started shortcutting arguments that we know the end of."

"Well, obviously that almost makes sense, but what if one of us walks away feeling hard done by and has to carry that around? That could build up into a resentment."

"Is there anything you want to get off your chest right now, before we close the door on it?"

She gave this some thought. Unfortunately, his logic had taken hold, and whenever she thought of something she wanted him to know had hurt her, she just realised it was definitely going to be one of the things they ended up letting go of. Why not just let go of it now and save yourself the time and trouble?"

"Are you sure this is a good idea? Because I kind of think it could end up creating more problems than it solves."

He looked at her with a smile that was not his warmest.

"See, what you are doing there, my love, is starting the argument."

"I'm not starting the argument. First of all, this whole thing was your idea, and therefore, if it is now an argument, it was you who started it, and second of all, this sounds like an excuse for you to hurt my feelings and then get away with it because we're not allowed to have arguments."

"Wow. There is so much in there that I want to disagree with."

"Why, because you want an argument?"

"No, because it's wrong. First of all, why would you say "get to" hurt your feelings, as though it were something I wanted to do; and second of all, nobody is saying you are "allowed" or not to do anything. I just thought, here we are, on the verge of an argument, it's a beautiful day - why don't I just suggest a way around it so we don't have to keep arguing all the time? I can see that is never going to work."

Two Six-Word Stories by Carl & Stephen

Supporting Leyton, an education in disappointment.

Retired pinball wizard, retraining for darts.

Welcome by Chris Bird

A week-old newspaper lay on the table in the dingy day room. I reached for it and settled into the least busy corner browsing now old Parliamentary scandals.

Opposite me, the kettle wheezed its way to boiling like an old car revving up. A service user rang the buzzer from the outside gate waiting to be let in by a volunteer.

The psychology students who made up the pool of volunteers on the main had a kind and yet lost quality.
They floated around greeting people with affected warmth.

"Cup of tea or coffee?" They asked as more people appeared heading towards the boiling kettle.

The far corner was Joe's corner. He fancied himself a boxer, swivelling and air punching quick jabs with little hisses of effort. Some days he stripped off his t-shirt, today fully clothed. Weaving from side to side he threw a big right hook. Another knockout victory.

In the corner by the window, it was kicking off. A dispute about someone sleeping on the sofa.
"Do one you idiot!" The formerly sleeping woman shouted.
"Have a cuppa and shut your trap," someone suggested.
"Keep ya nose out!" Came a barked reply.

An argument was boiling. I turned the page.

The Picnic by Hazel Norbury

Metin is waiting at the school gates as I come out of the cashier's office brandishing a wad of notes stuffed into a brown envelope. It is always awkward shaking hands with the manager as she hands over my monthly salary, almost double the amount she and her Turkish colleagues earn. He lights a cigarette and cricks his neck.

"I want to buy a new dolmuş. No one is using American cars in Adana now. Can you lend me some money for a deposit?"

New minibuses do not come cheap, even in Turkey. I shrug my shoulders, then removing just enough for food and basics, plus a few social outings over the next few weeks, I proffer the envelope. He snatches it, almost elbowing me in the process and thrusts it deep inside his jacket.

"I want this back by the end of next month, otherwise I'll charge you interest."
"Interest?" An unfamiliar concept. I explain the rate and the repayment period for defaulting on the loan. A whisper of smoke dribbles from the side of his mouth. He'll dine out on this for years to come.

Saturday morning and I open the door to a set of keys glinting in the hallway. Parked outside is the dolmuş, gleaming white, spotless windows revealing rows of beige leather seating and rubber matting on the floor, shiny like liquorice. I clamber in, the first passenger. We stop for several of my teaching colleagues and two American friends living off base in İncirlik. They pile in, easily accommodated, theatregoers taking their seats for the performance, the sense of occasion heightened by the privilege of being invited on a family outing.

Last of all, we pick up Grandma. Carrying a fair amount of weight, she's a bit unsteady on her feet and requires a push from Metin to get her inside. I wrinkle my nose as the smell of urine pervades the interior of the dolmuş. We all fall silent, not wishing to make her any more uncomfortable than she would be in the presence of so many strangers. 'Nasılsın, Grandma?' Metin tries to cajole her but elicits only a shuffling of feet. Twenty minutes beyond Adana, we turn off the main highway down a country lane. The dolmuş jolts over a rock, Metin swears and Grandma fills the footwell. The smell sours the air and I shove open the window nearest me and stick my head out, sipping the headwind. Others follow suit.

"Poor thing," someone says quietly and tuts.

"That is very naughty, Grandma!" Metin is more concerned with the puddle on the floor. We arrive at our destination and park up next to a dozen or so other cars. We jump out and Grandma tries to do a runner. Metin bursts into a sprint and leaps on her back, managing to wrestle her to the ground and then secures her in a headlock. Metin's parents appear with Selahattin, a young man who works summers in their pansion. Greetings are exchanged in a mixture of Turkish and English. Metin's mother, Gulseren, hands nylon headscarves to the women explaining this is a holy site and we need to be respectful. She helps me tie mine on, then fusses round the others ensuring there will be no slippage. As the men disappear with Grandma, we are left to contemplate our new selves, tucking in wayward strands of hair and tugging at the knots that which sits uncomfortably around our necks.
Several minutes elapse before Metin returns, his forehead dotted with beads of sweat. He is brandishing a large knife, its edge covered in dark cherry blood.

"You are my wife. You must put some above your nose to bless my dolmuş. It is tradition."

"I'm not your wife."

"You are like my wife." The blade comes closer. Invisible fingers prod me forward as, with everyone looking on expectantly, I dip my finger in and anoint my forehead with a single spot. The blood is surprisingly thick and still warm. Metin beams, utters a short prayer and then smears the rest over one of the dolmuş tyres.

The blessing over, Gulseren leads the way uphill to a picnic area. A large plastic tablecloth is unfurled over the grass; we help her unpack utensils, chopping boards, salad ingredients, bread, cheese and olives. I kneel next to her and translate as she directs the food preparation. I am assigned the honour of chopping a huge mound of flat leaf parsley as finely as possible, each scythe of the blade releasing an almost lemon sharpness. Grappling with the tangle of green stalks, I fail to notice the men have congregated beneath a large tree. Metin beckons me over, gesturing for me to bring a small knife. I am confronted by Grandma strung up and naked. In the void between her neck and groin I see the meat market in the old part of town where barrels piled high with lungs, heart and intestine soak up the thirty-six degree heat.

Metin takes the knife, makes a small nick in the skin near Grandma's feet and proceeds to blow up her legs like a balloon, one by one.

"This way the meat will dry out quicker," he explains, then to the amusement of his father, he licks his lips, grabs me in a bear hug and tries to kiss me.
I struggle free and run off back to the safety of washing and wiping, chopping and slicing. The men busy themselves with the barbecue as Grandma arrives on a large metal tray, reduced to tiny squares of shish which we thread onto skewers and sprinkle with cumin and paprika before carefully laying her over the grill. A beggar appears and Metin's father hands her a large chunk of meat he has kept aside for that purpose, explaining that it is customary to give to the poor. Despite his father's disapproval Metin has brought a crate of beer and a bottle of raki to enjoy alongside Grandma. As I chew down on her, I am reminded of having four teeth removed as a ten-year-old and all I can taste at the back of my throat is blood.

Gulseren's voice at first low and hesitant, suddenly gathers momentum and volume, a departure from custom and convention. I lean forward straining for familiar words and phrases.

"Mum says there is a famous women's cave here on this site. In our tradition, you find a small stone and place it on the holy rock at the bottom. If your stone sticks to the rock, you will be very lucky in your life."

We clap our thanks to Gulseren, savouring this new morsel of insight, of culture. A flash of pride precedes a flurry of plate clearing, signalling a return to the natural order of things. Metin raises his glass and proposes a toast to the dolmuş, and to Grandma.
"And to Gulseren," I add, instigating a second round of applause.

Metin bounds downhill, eager to show us the narrow entrance to the cave. In we go, scrambling down, deeper and deeper, our eyes adjusting to the lack of light until we find ourselves in a small chamber. Ahead of us, we hear numerous sighs of disappointment. When my turn comes, I scrabble round on the sandy floor and eventually unearth a tiny pebble. I press it to the rock's jagged surface and, holding my breath, slowly remove my hand. It stays put.

"I've done it! I've done it!" I whisper to my friends and then braver, "Yaptım! Yaptım!" eager to let all the women in the cave know. It's a sign. I am blessed. I belong here in this land with these people. I fall in behind three Turkish women beginning their ascent out of the cave, eager to ask if they're enjoying their day. The one nearest to me pauses to sniff the air and mutters 'Yabancı,' before she hacks and spits over her shoulder.
I lower my head and trudge upwards, propelled towards the sunshine by a familiar fleeting sadness.

Nan's Front Room by Webster Forrest

The stillness of my Nan's front room had never been so much as infringed upon in my lifetime, never mind shattered as it was now. The kids were swiftly ushered out; the pies were in the oven and the telly in the back room had just been switched on. Match of the Day. That should do the trick. I looked at Susan. She was the self-appointed putter of flowers into water. All of the usual vases had been used up before the service. Now, with all these extra flowers - who knows where they would go. Buckets perhaps. Or possibly a few branded pint glasses on the back step - those would be the ones people could take with them. The people for whom the pies baked.

They weren't here yet. Now it was just the tier-one mourners. The people who had actually watched her over the last six months. The ones who had cleaned up after her. The ones who had been in the room, on the night, when it happened. The ones who had seen her dead and kissed her goodbye while she was lukewarm.

The others would be there soon, though. They were the ones who needed to be provided with the

address, who had bought flowers online, rather than in shops where you get to see the ones you're getting. They weren't bad people, the second-tier mourners; they just weren't the ones who'd been there. In a way, it would have felt inappropriate if they had been there: out of scale, improprietous. They'd done the right thing by staying away, at a respectable distance before the death, when the death was an accepted eventuality.
That was the moment the gears began to turn. Arrangements had to be made, options selected and decisions made. Verses, chosen. Music.
Act I, scene I - Granny is Put in a Box…

The pies began to spread their aroma throughout the house. Nanna's bank account had had four hundred and seventeen pounds in it. That all got transferred out without incident. The correct forms had been filled in and lodged in due course. That part of it was seamless. The final collapse of that last arterial wall, though. That came with a bit of drama. Blood.

I looked at the houseplants she had on a frame in the light of her front window. For decades they had been the only living things that spent more than a few minutes a week in her front room; Grandad's presence still made itself felt there, though its palpability had faded over the years. The rotating beechwood pipe rack still got dusted, but the pipes themselves had gradually lost much of their sweet smokey aroma and the sooty black bowls had taken on a tarry acrid stench. Like Grandad before them, and now Granny too, they had gone from warm and aromatic to smelly and dead.

The first of the tier-two participants pulled up and parked their car a respectful distance from the drive; nobody would be able to accuse anybody of having blocked the drive. God knows what emergencies might befall them during the course of the afternoon. One of the tier-one lot might even have to do an ice cream run. Or go out for a fag. No smoking in the house.

Therapy by Chris Bird

Harriet spoke to us like a primary school teacher approaching recalcitrant kids. She was the new art therapist on the ward. Nurses had been encouraging patients to attend all morning. Our primary focus was lunch but 5 or 6 of us had joined the group in the day room.
She exuded liberal kindness.
Nathan beside me at the table stank of piss. An all-pervading pungent aroma. I couldn't move seat. The plastic chairs, like the tables, bolted to the floor. The narrow ward windows were also secured.
Had a fight once develop over the merits of watercolour compositions.

Paul looked uneasy, fidgeting in his chair, glancing at me. He had a ruthless streak when provoked. Mohammad sat opposite. He was a timid, emaciated character who could not stand up for himself in an empty room. He was being bullied on the ward.

"Can we have music, Miss?" Paul rumbled in a deep voice.
"No fucking way!" snapped Andrew.

Andrew claimed to be a gangster, a dealer.
Insisted we refer to him as 'Cobra'. The natural rival to Paul.
Harriet smiled to encourage peaceful co-existence.
Looking at her, I genuinely hoped no one kicked off.
I tried to smile back in a gesture of muted reassurance.

Paul shuffled, assessing the degree of threat from Cobra.
Once satisfied, hurled a plastic jug of water.
It sailed across the table, missing him but drenching Harriet.

M3 by Webster Forrest

"What's this old thing? It looks gross."

Ma looked over with a neutral expression then her mouth popped open and she reached both hands out. I passed it over to her.

"Well will you look at that - that's your dad's old camera."
She held it like a cat she was about to stroke.
"Where did you find this? He looked for that old thing for about a month a while back."

"It was just here in this box."

"Which box?"

I showed her. It was a shoebox but it must have been from some pretty fancy shoes; it was a lot nicer than the boxes my shoes come in.
"He used to love this camera. He took beautiful pictures with it. Oh, he had it with him all the time back in those days."

My father had been blind throughout my entire life - the result of a chemical accident at the plant where he worked. His eyes were all scarred and he used to wear these huge glasses to hide them. I only ever saw his real eyes a few times. I had no idea he had ever been interested in photography.

I looked at my mother. She was gazing at this old camera. She had a way of holding anything precious by only the tips of her fingers that made it seem weightless. She eventually looked up at me. She had the sort of expression that people have when they are holding a baby, and then they look up to look at you, and their face has, 'isn't this wonderful' written all over it.

Suddenly her expression changed. She appeared to be zeroing in on something. She turned the camera over in her hands then pulled up a knurled little knob at one end of it and rotated it slightly with her fingers. Then she sat back and grinned at the ceiling.

She looked over at me, then declared,
"It's still got film in it, Doogie. Your father's last ever roll of film is in this camera. Look - there's thirty-two exposures on this roll. We have to get it developed. Right now."

"Do people even still do that? That photo lab in the mall has been closed since I was in high school."
"Son - I've got a job for you. Go and look up film developing or photographic services and find somewhere we can take this roll of film. It has to be today. They have to be open today.'

I went to the other room and got a drink then sat looking for somewhere on my phone. After only a few minutes she appeared in the doorway in her coat.
'Have you found it?', she asked.

'Uh, there's a few places in here.' I started reading out the names of the photographic businesses I'd found. Suddenly she stopped me and came up to look over my shoulder.

'Jameson's on Elm - that's the place your father used to take his film. We're going there. Come on - get your coat.'

'Do you want the address?'

'Don't need it; been there a million times.'

We all but ran out to the car and screeched the tires as we raced off to Jameson's Photographic.

We got there in no time. My mother seemed more alive than she had for ages - at least since dad got sick. She knew the way and we walked right in.

There was one of those little brass bells on a contraption over the door and it made a pleasant single ring when we entered. A good-looking young guy was behind the counter and looked up. There were a few tables, and a coffee machine. For a moment I thought we were out of luck, but then I saw all the photographic prints on the walls and noticed a big unit back of the counter that had these shelves that were kind of like pigeonholes except they were all on a forty-five-degree angle and contained hundreds of small cardboard boxes of different kinds of film stock. My mom was at the counter like a bat outta hell.

"Hello there, my name is Helen Blackstone, my husband Artie used to bring all his films here for development. Do you still develop films here?"

The young man smiled - he seemed to like something about my mother, her very forward energy perhaps.

"Yes, ma'am, we do indeed. What sort of film do you need developed?"

My mom produced the camera from her purse and put it on the counter. The young guy reached out and picked it up. He seemed to like it very much and handled it carefully.

"Artie died yesterday. We've been going through his things, and my son - c'mere Doogie - this is my son Doogie - Doogie found his camera."

Mom grasped my hand without looking and held on to it.

"If you turn the rewind thing you'll feel…" He was doing this and nodding at the same time. "…that there's still a roll of film in there."

"And you say your late husband used to come in here with his films?"

"Oh gosh yes, for years Artie came in here. Must have developed a few rolls of film a week for, well for years and years. That was until his accident. My husband was blind for the last twenty-seven years of his life."

She looked in my face and I saw she was going to cry. I put my arm around her and kissed the top of her head. She spoke through tears, saying, "And so, we would like to find what these pictures are in his camera. Can you do that for me, son?"

The boy behind the counter looked at her with a kindness that made me feel he was a nice person. He took some time before he spoke. I watched his eyes as he spoke with my mother. He had large dark brown eyes that were very striking.

"Would you mind if I made a quick phone call? I just need to ask my father a couple of questions about this order, because the film has been undeveloped so long."

"Oh, do you think it will be ruined by now?"

"If we're in luck it will be black and white, in which case, possibly not. Do you know how long the film has been in the camera?"

"Since March 7th, 1998."

The young man nodded silently, smiled at me, and went into the back. A moment later a young lady came out and silently ushered us to one of the little tables. She brought us coffee and some little sweets to eat. The coffee was delicious, and this little shop was nice and warm. Mom sat at the little table in her coat and looked around at the pictures on the walls. For the first time since dad's death it felt like she was alive, though her mood was very calm.

After about ten minutes the little bell above the door jingled, and we both looked up. An old man with grey hair and large dark eyes came in. My mother seemed to transform into a different age, and the man came up to us with a charming smile.

"Mrs. Blackstone, how lovely to see you."

"Oh - Mr. Tom, I can't believe my eyes - is it really you?"

They stood shaking both hands together for a long moment.

"Mr. Tom, this is my son Doogie."

"Ah! I can see the resemblance - you look just like your father."

He turned to my mother. "How is Mr. Blackstone?"

"Artie died yesterday. Oh, Mr. Tom, he would be so glad to know we were here - and it never would have happened but for Doogie found his old camera!"

"Yes, I understand you have a film to develop. May I see the camera?"

We went over to the countertop and all four of us crowded around the old camera.
"Oh - can't develop."

My mother's face dropped.

"Still has four unexposed frames in it," he said. "Come." He led us outside.

The young man and the girl followed. Mr. Tom took out a lens cloth and cleaned the front of the lens, then using an exposure meter he produced from his pocket - it was on his keychain - he set the exposure on the camera and showed the girl how to focus it. The four of us stood for portraits together in front of the shop. My mother, myself, Mr. Tom, and his son.

"'Now it's ready," he said with a smile. "It will take about an hour. Would you like to wait here and have coffee, or would you like to come back?"

We waited inside the little shop and had coffee and talked about dad and his interest in photography. I learned that he wanted to become a professional at one point, but when he lost his sight, he never wanted to discuss it again. Mom said he was not bitter about losing his sight, because it was just a sheer dumb accident caused by a faulty component and wasn't anybody's fault, but he thought that if he were to give any thought to photography after that point, he would become bitter over time, and so the subject was officially made taboo by my parents. I never knew a single thing about any of this.

After about an hour Mr. Tom came out with a big stack of 8x10 prints. The pictures were black and white, and I was impressed at how crisp and dark the blacks were, and how the whites were bright and clean, but retained detail, nevertheless. They were from a family holiday and then a barbecue. I knew from other pictures that this was the holiday home they used to have in Florida. I remember finding out about that place when I was in high school and being mad at them that they had had a getaway place in the sun and had sold it without thinking it would be good for when I got older.

Strangest for me was seeing for the first time photographs of my father from before he lost his sight. I guess a lot changed after his accident - he sort of wiped out the past, I guess.

I held one picture up and looked at it very closely. In it my father was looking straight into the lens. It must have been my mom who had taken the picture, because the only people in it were my father and me as a toddler. He was holding me in his hands, kind of like how people used to hold babies. I tried to read the look on his face but there was some kind of mental block to doing so. It didn't really feel like that was my father. I never saw my father's eyes.

Finally, it came to the last pictures on the roll - the ones we had just taken. Mr. Tom had chosen the best one and made an extra copy. He took it and walked over to the wall where there was an empty spot among the other framed photographs and held it up there then looked at my mother with a questioning smile. She gave him the thumbs up.

We took the photographs home, along with the developed film. Mr. Tom kept the camera and said he would have a friend of his do a full service on it. I wasn't sure what the purpose of that was, but the old man was very insistent.

A couple of weeks later he turned up at the house. My mum invited him in and we sat down in the kitchen dining area and had coffee and he told me all about how to use the camera, which I learned was a Leica M3, which was meant to be a really good camera. It certainly felt very solid and well made, and now that it was all cleaned up it was very nice to look at too.

About a week later I was sitting around with nothing to do, and I started fiddling around with my dad's old camera. The controls were so smooth, and it had a way of just sitting in your hands and making you feel you had the power to go out and take beautiful pictures. And when you pressed the button it made the most beautiful quiet sound, like someone sliding a card up off a table with a snap. I put the strap round my neck and called out to my mum that I was going for a walk.

There was a disused old brewery near the park that I thought might yield some cool pics.

At least I would know where to get the film developed.

Human Dilemmas
CW: mental health

That Beautiful Town

Sidmouth in Devon,
Nestled between red cliffs by the sea;
Catches both rain and sun
Has long been a home for my family and me.

Pretty and brightly coloured,
with deckchairs on the promenade.
Small cafes offer up a variety of cream teas.
To leave there is very hard people say.

Gardens galore -
Connaught, Blackmore, Peak hill;
Plus Jacob's ladder to climb.
It lies along the Jurassic Coast not so still.
The waves lap and intermingle
with sand and waiting shingle.

Temporal Lobe Epilepsy

Why do you put yourself in my brain? For what reason exactly? It is MY brain, MY mind, MY life, not yours. Why can you not understand that and leave me alone?

I do not want the memories or rather déjà vu you give me; I cannot handle you taking away my power and independence of thought and experience. You open up my brain when I am asleep and insert future happenings and memories there despite knowing it will freak me out.

You make me smell gas when there is not any around, you put a taste of metal in my mouth and a physical sensation there that is hard to describe. You enter my chest with a heaviness that is so hard to shift. You invade my body and my mind and take them over. I refuse to let you control me and yet you still do.

Please go away and leave me in peace. Let go of my brain and let it just be mine again. I do not want your future memories; I just want my life back.

Depersonalisation

Depersonalisation, along with derealisation, is part of the illness Chronic Dissociative Disorder but can also occur under extreme stress, as part of a temporal lobe epileptic seizure and also a symptom of some mental health diagnoses – for example, Emotionally Unstable (Borderline) Personality Disorder.

The mind divorces itself from the body, it is literally a case of "Oops I lost my mind today." My mind can trot off goodness knows where – Mars? – leaving an empty body, brain and mind.

Unfortunately, it leaves behind any unpleasant emotions I may be feeling and also incites panicky feelings at the realisation of my being's departure takes hold. My brain is simultaneously busy with emotion yet hollow; my being has left my body behind to somehow carry on by itself.

Enter robot-come-actress mode. Fake robot Madeleine takes over, tries to act it out as my real self. Amazingly, I can fool most people that I am still a real human being but a handful of those close to me know better… "There's a distant look in your eyes, you are not quite here," they say. I am enormously grateful to these few people and feel I can relax in front of them and just be, or rather, 'not be'.

Sometimes, for example, when having a large seizure, the depersonalisation comes in huge overwhelming swathes which make me feel like I have been knocked over by a tidal wave. No acting then! Indeed, no talking, I am literally taken over by an assault of emptiness and fear.

This disorder has become a very regular part of my life, hours and hours and hours of it every day and I have rarely found anyone else who experiences it as well. One thing I would love to know is where my mind really does go when it disappears? (I joke Mars but surely not). Also why is it so fractured?

Post-Traumatic Stress Disorder

Inadvertently I turned the radio on at one minute to the hour and the news began several seconds later. Boom! A major car accident was the headline, and in my panic to turn off the radio I haphazardly hit all sorts of buttons, receiving various stations similar reports.

When the radio finally went quiet, the room was not. My now tachycardic heartbeats were so loud I could hear them outside of my chest. Looking down I could see its rapid rise and fall, plus my shaking legs and unstill hands.

Inside my brain a menacing black car drove at speed towards a figure on a pavement; to my horror it was me. As the flashback reached its climax my head thankfully blocked it out just in time.

In an effort to calm myself I got up off the sofa and nearly fell over in my haste to reach my handbag. "Where's the fucking diazepam?" I screamed into the empty room.

By now I was both sweating yet shivering and could feel a recent meal rise up to my throat.

Flashback, rapid heartbeat, shaking limbs. A strip with six yellow pills left. I decided two should be taken at once. There was no water in the lounge so I swallowed them quickly with the dregs of an old coffee.

"Bloody radio… stop!!"

As was common, I could not say the full words out loud. Oh they pinged around inside my head often and easily enough, alongside gruesome images. The vast majority of my time as taken up with the mental consequences to the trauma I had gone through. However to say certain relevant words and describe out loud what was constantly re-lived was impossible. I could not speak to a counsellor and I was sure I frustrated my psychiatrist.

Every day I was afraid to see or listen to the news in case it provoked it. Friends knew better than to mention the subject in my presence. Getting outside and even walking down the inside of the pavement presented massive problems. I had been signed off work as the disorder dominated my life, even sleep held it's reminders of my traumatic experience.

I felt peace would never come again. All attempts in dating had failed. Instead I ate, drank and smoked too much in the search for comfort.

Often housebound, usually alone, music had become a friend. These days it was soft, classical melodies that I craved; no pop nor dramatic tunes. Occasionally a bit of light jazz. I popped a gentle jazz C.D. in the machine.

I sighed; the double Diazepam was not working yet. I was still in crisis. If it was possible to talk I would. For now I listened to the music and closed my eyes

The Decision

The slam of the front door pierced Emma's semiconsciousness and moved her from dozing to fully awake in an instant. Some mornings she would barely register the auditory intrusion; such was her need and desire for sleep, she would simply turn over and sink into unconsciousness again. However not today. Eyes wide open, she lay back against the pillows and listened out, somewhat anxiously, for other sounds. Birds tweeted in the communal back garden, an ambulance's siren could be heard in the distance amongst vague traffic noises; that was all. Emma's increased heart rate slowly started to subside, no Benji noises yet. Not that her baby usually roused before 7:30am giving her another half hour to herself.

Good mums, she thought, *would use that time to get ready for the day.* Shower, dress, or prepare bottles, or… Emma felt the familiar sense of lethargy and inertia filter through her. With Matthew departed for work her day was laid out ahead of her. It would be eleven hours before her husband was home and today was only Tuesday? Wednesday…? She shook her head in annoyance at her inability -

increasingly common these days - to remember simple things like days and dates.

Some short time later, a wail sprung up from the room next door. Emma's eyes darted immediately to the clock. 7:20am. "Benji, you're early."

The wailing grew louder; more irritable. Benji's mother pushed aside her warm bed covers and made her way into his nursery. She was greeted with a red, blotchy, wretched-looking face, peppered with tears and a little wrinkled frown.

Overcome with guilt and empathy, Emma picked up her son and cradled him hard against her cheek, rocking the pair of them to and fro. "I'm sorry, little one. Mummy should have come."

An odour of diarrhoea assaulted her nostrils as she nestled him, giving reason for his now unusually vitriolic crying. "Alright Benji, mummy will sort you out, you'll soon be clean again."

Although the words were meant well, Emma's heart was sinking at the thought of what she would have to go through to restore hygiene on her son.

"Where are you when I bloody need you?!" She screamed into the room, causing Benji to look at her in shock and start screaming himself.

"Oh shit. Oh shit, oh shit-oh! Literally!" she said clutching and rocking her child and feeling his sodden babygrow as for the first time.

Emma desperately thought for the advice that both her GP and her counsellor had given her.
Do things one at a time. Take deep breaths. Don't forget to take your pills.
With her hands full of her baby and his poo, grabbing an anti-depressant or a diazepam was out of the equation. Emma started to inhale and exhale as thoroughly and slowly as possible. Benji began to scrutinise his mother with interest.

Reaching a more settled, less anxious point after a few minutes, Emma proceeded to slowly undress, clean and redress her little boy. She knew she should have given him a bath but also knew she could not manage the rigmarole of that. Better a box of baby wipes and the reliance that a five-month-old would not tell on her.

Benji sat contentedly in his baby chair watching the Disney channel. Emma lay behind him on the sofa, curled up in a familiar foetal position, eyes mostly closed but fluttering half open now and then to check on her baby. Closed curtains and dimmed lights struck a contrast against the flashes and colourful scenes of The Jungle Book. Benji gurgled. Emma felt the weight of pain and depression reside in her stomach, a ton that had been there since the diarrhoea incident earlier that day, and maybe almost since the day Benjamin had been born.

She regarded herself as such a bad mother, she would say pathetic but that didn't cover it. *Good mums play with their children. Good mums take their kids to the park or to groups. Good mums fucking bathe their kids when they poo everywhere!* Emma practically screeched this last thought out loud causing Benji to jolt in his seat and whimper momentarily.

Today, for good or bad, was a day without any appointments. No GP, no counsellor, no baby checks. Emma however felt relieved; it meant just hiding out in the flat. Not having to face anyone who might just judge her. She knew she should sterilise most of the bottles - they were running very low - and to do a couple of loads of laundry.

Those realisations upped her anxiety levels again. Whenever there were chores to be done, she would feel a sense of desperation, panic looming. She'd mostly leave the jobs for Matthew to do in the evenings, but she had started to sense his impatience about this recently.

Almost from the start Matthew had been brilliant about her post-natal depression and how viciously it was affecting her. He seemed to understand her feelings and reactions, despite them being so radically different to his own. She had been so hesitant to cuddle their infant, yet Matthew had been endlessly encouraging and gently supportive, never pushing her.

He had helped out whenever he could, including initially taking time off work and then working from home when possible. Even though he was now back at the office full time, she knew he'd more than pulled his weight.

However, these past few days, Emma had started to detect an undertone of annoyance in his voice at her inability to still not achieve virtually anything.

Why is he changing? Doesn't he love me anymore? Is he fed up with me as a bad mother to Benji?

She worried now. Curled up on the sofa, the thoughts churned in her head as she tried to analyse her husband's recent subtle changes of reaction. Had he really had enough? Was he that angry with her weeping state?

Emma dangled first one then two legs off the sofa, slowly coming to a sitting position, and then rubbed her eyes with her fingers to refresh herself. Time to do something. If pleasing Matthew meant sterilising the bottles, even tidying up a bit, then Emma determined to do it. It was time to take charge. The doctor had reassured her she was on the right medication (Emma pondered that one often) and the counsellor, Jane, was a good listener, so it was time for her, the patient, to try her bit again too.

Emma checked Benji was happy and secure and then made her way resolutely to the kitchen. A scattering of dirty dishes and baby bottles littered the worktop. She shuddered. The sight looked so much to overcome but she was determined to try.

A gathering headache started to settle on Emma's brow. Heart slightly pounding, she knelt down and opened the dishwasher, realising it was already full with clean crockery. Damn, it would need emptying first.

Faced with this, Emma felt skittish and unnerved and slipped down on the floor. She sat there, not moving or making a sound. She could actually hear her heart beat in her chest. Could she really manage all of this…? Emma was not even certain she could get back up off the floor.

In the lounge, The Jungle Book was becoming boring to Benji's young mind, he was beginning to wriggle in the bouncy chair and utter some moaning sounds. Hearing them, his mother put her head in her hands and began to sob. The tears poured down Emma's face tasting salty as they passed her lips, eventually causing her to hiccough.

Across the passageway, she became more conscious of Benji's sobs matching her own but was unable to comfort either of them. Time passed and mother and son eventually became spent, with just a gentle cough and cry occasionally from each.

Unsteadily, Emma rose to her feet and, feeling her way, walked to the living room where she found her son in a sodden, snotty state. A big pang of guilt struck her, she immediately picked him up and wrapped her arms protectively around his small torso.

"There, there, Benji, it's all over now. It's okay, mummy and you will be fine… shh".

His sad, sleepy eyes looked up at her. She was sure it was an accusing look. Stomach swimming with guilt and depression, Emma kissed her son's forehead and uttered more words of comfort, whilst feeling useless.

It was an hour before Matthew returned home. Benji had a new nappy and top on and had all of the last milk available. Propped on a cushion on his play mat, watching its mobile and listening to a CD of nursery rhymes, he seemed contented and settled again. Emma perched on the edge of the settee, contemplating a Bacardi and cola, another diazepam or both.

Today had been a particularly stressful day with no jobs done that she could show off to Matthew about. *Would he be annoyed?* The dirty kitchen, its dishes, the untidy lounge, the un-bought shopping, the lack of outing or bath for their baby son…

Not that Emma had showered or bathed herself. That was too much of a headache. She was approximating a short shower with a hair wash every five days now; occasionally mini washes in between. One quick visit to the hairdressers since Benji's birth but none to the beautician. Nobody, not even her counsellor understood how much of an effort everything was. Getting up was so hard and the days would go downhill thereafter. To wash and change her clothes felt like climbing a mountain, often needing a couple of sit downs in-between.

Coping with an infant son frequently seemed insurmountable and Emma had little practical daytime help. Her parents lived in Cumbria; Matthew's mother was deceased and his father had retired to Spain before they wed. Matthew's sister worked full time and was clueless about babies. Emma's brother and his wife had two young girls and tried to help but also lived in Cumbria. Besides, she had tried to hide the enormity of her post-natal depression from the family.
The GP and nurse kept informing her of suitable groups; however she was usually too tired and anxious to go outside the flat and also didn't want

professionals to see her and Benji together. She loved him, what if they were to take him away?

Emma got up and poured herself a double rum and cola and took a big gulp. She felt an unexpected urge for nicotine. Resisting as she hadn't had a cigarette for eighteen months and there were none on the house anyway, she sat back down and drank the dark liquid and for a moment mused… If only she had known how different in reality being a mother would have become to her dreams of it, if somebody had just warned her.

Her few parental friends and colleagues had been excited for Matthew and Emma, congratulated them, joking only about sleepless nights and a bit of teething; words like 'depression' 'apathy' 'sheer terror', and she shuddered to admit 'difficulty in bonding' had never been mentioned.

In that moment, Benji's mother knew she could not continue anymore. She looked down at her old jeans and coffee stained T-shirt, then across to the still curtained windows. Thoughts of the filthy kitchen made her inwardly shudder and she remembered that she had not made the bed yet.

"Enough," she said, "I can hardly manage one thing, let alone them all.'

The psychiatrist Dr Bower's voice came back to her in recollection.
"…If all else fails, there is always hospital, Emma. You can get a proper rest, good meals and the psychiatrist and nurses will be there for you, they will listen and talk to you. You can even take Benjamin on your stay."

"No!" Emma sat up straight, nearly spilling her drink.

She would go, she saw that clearly now, but just as clearly that she would go alone. She loved Benji, but she needed to escape him as much as the flat, her life, everything.

Relief spread through her, much like the rum had done ten minutes beforehand. For a moment or two, Emma actually felt relaxed. RELAXED!

Five months of struggling and all she could still manage was to dress herself in dirty old clothes and implement the most basic care for her baby.

Her baby? Benji did not feel like hers all that often, she sometimes admitted to herself. She never said that to anyone else though. What would people think? Did she care what people thought anymore though? She wondered and was not sure.

In an uncharacteristic burst of energy, Emma jumped up, she drained the glass and went to wash and dry the evidence, before cleaning her teeth and even brushing her hair.

Re-realising how dirty the kitchen surfaces were, the thought occurred to her that her husband might have left them like that on purpose. To provoke a reaction? To shock, force, will her into doing some housework? The earlier relaxation frittered away leaving familiar tension and worry instead.

How could you Matthew? I thought you more than anyone else comprehended the situation. Obviously not!

Entering the lounge, she caught sight of Benji's smile as he moved his gaze from the mobile to his mother.

Why are you pleased to see me, thought Emma.

I'm a shitty mum and now I even have plans to leave you for a while. You poor bugger - you really have no idea do you…

Kneeling, she tenderly stroked his head and arms, evoking more giggles and smiles. Wishing it could always be like this between them. Guilt crept into their tender moment. God, she loved him. At least most of the time she recognised. She worried about him a lot too. Yet here she was making plans to leave him and Matthew.

"Temporarily," she whispered. "Just until I'm right again. How long would that take? One week? Two? A month or more?"

Suddenly she wondered who would take care of their baby while Matthew worked.

"Never mind that, there are friends, my brother, Annie; someone will help out surely." She refused to allow the rising thought of social services to properly enter her mind.

Emma looked at her watch. 5:45pm, fifteen minutes until Matthew was due home. No jobs had or, realistically, could have been done. Just another day gone. That was an achievement in itself. A tough but clear decision had been reached: tomorrow she would call Dr Bower's office and ask for him to telephone her. Twice she had seen him and twice he had seemed kind and willing to help. *So let him,* she thought.

Benjamin was starting to get agitated, moaning. Emma panicked.

"Please, please Benji. Daddy's nearly home now. Stay good for five minutes baby!" She hated it when Benji was crying when Matthew returned, it made her feel even more worthless than usual. She patted his back and stuck a dummy in, it worked. As Benji quietened down a key could be heard in the door.

Emma relaxed for the second time that day. She could set down the tools of responsibility now and for longer than an evening as well. She had made her decision; she knew she'd stick to it even if she faced opposition.

Whilst hating to admit she was sick, she was not stupid. Emma took a deep breath and went to greet her husband.

Transmissions

CW: mental health, drug abuse, homelessness

Smoke

I

I thought about the city skyline.
Tower blocks, spires, skyscrapers and domes
scratched out on the side of a lit cigarette.
Grey shadows became ashes, wide swerving entities
of smoke stretching away like autobahns.
If you watch the embers long enough,
the strength of heroin overwhelms.

II

I pulled out a broken fag from my pocket.
Laid some cardboard on the pavement and sat.
The traffic choked the wide avenue.
Tube stations gorged on commuters.
Junkies filling up with grey smoke.
This was my skyline.

Street Signs

Polluted air billowed around me
as I cut across the road.
Hoardings advertised long-gone movies.
Darth Vader looking out through grime
reminded me of an interstellar Satan.

Beside an open iron gate
bins were over flowing.
Under some crude graffiti,
I noticed a discarded syringe:
a street sign.

I was in the right place.

The Walk

Even in summer,
King's Cross looked bleached and grim.
The walk back to Lincoln Inn Fields
was going to be a challenge.
The gear was in my left sock,
it was hard to believe it took a crumpled £50 to get.

I noticed a sticker on a lamppost,
a white 'A' symbol on a black/red background.
Anarchist concepts had always attracted me,
but I had become apathetic in the grips of gear.
My days now defined by the search for smack
or the cash to buy it.

I recognised a girl who haunted King's Cross.
She must have guessed that I was 'holding'.
"A yu gona be a pal?" she hissed.
I hurried past,
lending a thumbs up gesture that fell empty.
I heard her curse me in the distance.

When I reached the park I was pouring with sweat.
My t-shirt stuck to my skin,
I wanted to tear it off.
The park was too busy, every bench full.
I could see my tent in the distance.
I was nearly there.

Hush

Outside the park, I walked in a daze.
Unmedicated, hearing murmurs around me.
I made flaying, wheeling strokes
with my arms like a crazed windmill.

            A "hush" technique I'd learnt.

The voices abated.
They soon showed up again.
Leaping down from branches,
catching me in their web:

"88 slide."
"Invisible remote control."
"You hate them."
"So far for what?"

Slow Motion

Jim gave me a cigarette.
A sordid blessing from a corrupt priest.
I needed confidence,
it was my turn.

"Go Superdrug, get something pricey,"
he ordered.
I was pants at thieving,
scruffy and self-conscious.

I skirted around the perfume boxes,
bound with grenade-like tags.
In front of me were rows of deodorant.
That wouldn't impress Jim.

The staff were distracted,
the moment would soon pass.
I took a box,
anticipating a blaring alarm.

On my return, I braced myself
to show Jim what I had nicked.

"Toothpaste!" He spluttered derisively,
looking angry then bursting into laughter.

"And it was on special offer, you clown!"
He smiled with ragged teeth.

Sanctuary

Heroin looms over an addict
like a psychotically single-minded ghost.
For street users, it distorts reality.

Hurrying gaunt figures with cheap mobiles
hunt their source of utopia.
A sheltered spot from watching eyes,
small quantities traded for crumpled notes.
It's always fleeting.

Eating, keeping clean, even warm,
are far down the list of needs.
It's seedy, yet the hit is ethereal brilliance.

Heroin Will Mislead You

Sometimes
the warm glow of satisfaction
lasts for hours.
Loneliness negated, solved.
Aspirations cooled and reduced
to the miniature concept
of scoring again.
Heroin is a demanding drug.
It's jealous.
Devouring heart and soul,
it is the best and worst.

There I Go

As I held out the packet,
Jim looked with ferocity at my offering
in the gloom of the tent.
He snatched it,
slumping onto the dirty mattress.
"You can fuck right off!" He growled.

He'd sent me,
ordered me really,
up to Kings Cross to buy smack.
On the walk there I lost a tenner,
throwing away our hard-begged money.

As I walked in the park I felt utterly alone.
A street lamp projected a dirty-yellow light.
I wanted to step into that discoloured glow
and disappear.

Puppet

A reluctant vein bulged beneath pale skin
as I pulled the cord on his arm.
In his hand the syringe looked clean, harmless;
a throwaway indiscretion.

"Ok," said Jim.
For a moment everything froze.
He backed into the mattress and closed his eyes.
A trace of blood along his pale arm.

I sat back and lit a fag, looking at Jim.
A skinny mannequin doll,
laying in an odd, ungainly position.
His legs kicked out involuntarily.

He started mumbling, struggling to get up.
I offered him my cigarette.
I could taste nicotine on my lips as I whispered,
"Now me."

They Came from The Shadows

Like a chav light brigade, they charged.
Cursing booze-muddled words.
In that moment the evening shattered.

The attackers as young as joyriders,
vindictive as Nazis.
Brave with cheap lager and speed.

I caught a glimpse of white trainers
kicking at the flimsy tents.
The tents gave up easily.

In a whirl of bitter giggles and drunken bravado,
The attackers were gone.
Silence.

Our Side

Fluorescent orange waistcoats loaded the lorry.
They cleared the tents without looking at us,
muttering to one another.

Jim and I stood on the path, a pathetic air about us.
Jim, Sal and I'd been staying in the park for
months.
We'd been given the tents by a Hindu charity.

The park warden watched like a cut-price
lieutenant
overseeing the eviction. A distracted police officer
stood beside him, they both exuded disinterest.

"Crunch" went the tents as they folded in on
themselves.
Our camp disposed of as if litter.
A murder of crows screeched, disturbed by the
upheaval.

Slowly each day, the feathers came emerging from the skin of my hands and shoulders. I kept this discovery hidden knowing it was the key to my escape

A Medic's Journey to the Falklands

CW: body injury

A Medic's Journey to the Falklands
by Leslie Aldridge

My birth mother, Esther Finch, was nineteen years old when she gave birth to me in June 1960. At the time she was living at home with her mother and working as a poorly paid cleaner in an Ipswich hospital. She named me Leslie after my father. I know nothing of him other than he was called George Leslie Gladstone, was somewhat older than my mother, was already married and came from Jamaica.

Shortly after I was born, Esther was diagnosed with a brain tumour. She asked her mother to help look after me, I was told that her response was "I'm not going to look after that little black thing."

With Esther being ill at the age of three months, I was given up for adoption and was taken in by Dr Barnardo's.

I lived at the Princess Alice School children's home in Sutton, Coldfield until at the age of eight from where I was fostered by John and Joan Aldridge who became Dad and Mum.

John was a social worker at the school. Joan later worked as an occupational health assistant. In 1970, when I was ten, John found employment as

Head Gardener at a psychiatric hospital in Staffordshire.
We moved from our small house to a large semi-detached house close to the hospital. As the house gate and front door were open, patients would invite themselves in. I remember the occasional patient putting cigarette ash on the carpet.

Every fortnight I would go to Ashby-de-la-Zouch to see my dad's parents of which I have fond memories.
I found the early days of my primary school quite hard as I was newly adopted and did not like my mum. I was given tasks to do like scrub the kitchen floor, she would not be happy with my cleaning and grab me under the arm, leaving nail impressions in my skin.
On many occasions coming home from school I would go to the local shop and buy a box of matches, some sausages and a newspaper, thinking I could run away. Mum asked a female police officer to speak to me. She said if I continued to run away, I would be put in a children's home, this warning from the police stopped me trying to run away.
As I got older my dad and I put a "Mirror" yacht together. The yacht came in kit form, and we

assembled it together in the garage down the road where my dad had allotment. Once the yacht was assembled, we would strap it to the roof of the car and go sailing.

I enjoyed secondary school, particularly rugby, football and cross country as I was good at them. I was also very interested in history. I embarked on the Duke of Edinburgh Award scheme and attended a course at Hanley police station which led me into trying to get into the police force, unfortunately, I wasn't tall enough.

I left school at sixteen and while I awaited my results dad got me a job in the hospital on the cleaning team. I became interested in working as a nursing cadet at the hospital after seeing a poster outside the nursing office. However, as I did not have an interest in psychiatric nursing, I went to the Stoke on Trent Royal Navy information office to apply to become a medical assistant in the Navy. I took the entrance exam in September 1976 but failed the maths. My parents arranged private maths tuition for me and in October I retook the exam and passed.

On the morning of the 22nd of March 1977, I joined the Navy. Whilst waiting to catch the train to Plymouth I met Phillip. He was joining the Medical

Branch as a laboratory technician. We were to do our training together at HMS Raleigh. This was a training establishment for all new recruits.

About fifteen of us, shared a mess. A loudspeaker would awaken us for breakfast followed by parade ground fitness drills then lessons. After six weeks at HMS Raleigh before had our passing out parade which our parents attended.

After a weekend with my parents, we were taken by coach to Gosport, Hampshire to join Royal Naval Hospital Haslar where I undertook my Stage Two and Three training. Stage Two training took 8 weeks, the Stage Three took 8 months.

In Stage Two we learned about pharmacy, first aid, nursing, service administration and attended naval chemical defence training. After eight weeks training, we qualified and were awarded, in accordance with the Geneva Convention, our Red Cross to sew onto our right arm.

Stage Two training had been good, Phillip and I had gone for weekends home to Stoke-on-Trent. He died of leukaemia aged 27. Over the years I would visit him in the Royal Naval Cemetery in Gosport. His tombstone has his official Naval Number on that is three numbers away from mine.

Part Three training was on the wards, I have memories of spending my first week of Stage Three training learning how to test urine. I laugh when I look back as I remember thinking is this what I'm destined to. I worked on several wards but found I had an interest in the dressing ward where I would deal with wounds, and found I enjoyed suturing. After months of ward reports and assessments I was a confirmed and qualified medical assistant. I was asked to go for an internship in Southampton Eye Hospital and was awaiting a start date when war broke out. We were informed to pack service cases as we would be going to the Falklands. At that point I had been in the Navy five years but not been to sea.

On the morning of April 19th 1982, we loaded into coaches and taken to Brize Norton. The coach I was on had several members of my nursing class on it, the very first-time women had been at sea with the Navy. We were bundled into a Hercules and flown to Gibraltar.
At RNH Gibraltar we worked storing the ship (SS Uganda) with medical equipment and supplies. All medical staff, doctors and nurses formed rows to pass stores from the shore onto the ship. We worked hard over the weekend and, on Monday, set sail.

On the voyage to the Falklands, we were all designated jobs. I was to work in the triage area near the back of the ship where we would receive casualties. We spent time practicing triage, the formation of an operating theatre, creating a burns assessment, treatment ward and psychiatry ward, which I helped set up. As soon as that was done, I was taken back to the triage area.

In the early evening of May 4th 1982, the loudspeaker came on to announce that HMS Sheffield - a type 42 destroyer - has been hit by the Argentinian air force and badly damaged. We knew then we were in a war.
By May 14th we were receiving casualties from the forces engaged on the ground on both sides. We were working around the clock looking after them. Many had foot wounds, others penetrating injuries, amputees and burns.
On June 8th we received casualties from the Sir Tristan and Sir Galahad. These were Welsh guards that had full body burns. They suffered terribly and were put in the burns ward at the front of the ship. The burns ward is an area which I will have memories of for the rest of my life. The injuries were horrifying. Men were in terrific pain, with their arms elevated on drip stands in plastic bags

covered in Flamazine, a cream to give the burns hopefully less chance of scarring.

The smell and the noise of the pain those men were in will be with me for life. I was so tired at the end of each day from this work that thankfully I was able to sleep and, at the time, blank out the horror of it all…

*This section is a truncated version of A Medic's Journey to the Falklands, edited by Tom Mallender with Leslie's permission

Lost Letters

The Almond Tree by Naino Masindet

At smallest shadow
I met with a winter's oath
Forged from the earth
The bluest blood and vein

Its sweet honeyed blossom
That falls gently down
Preserved by creeping frost,
A gravestone kiss

Beneath a watercolour sky,
Branches of love's martyr
Burdened with despair
Until their newborn breath

In my humble garden
Of white violets and aconites,
I write upon the hour
I met with the almond tree.

The Architecture of Escape by Naino Masindet

Be still with me
Like a lingering cloud
When I am lost in the heart of you
Forever kept like a souvenir,
A keychain with my name on.

Whilst you awaken adagio
And a soft string dawn echoes
Through my trembling bones
You teach me how to fiercely colour you outside
the lines

Sunken cobblestone
Under a mercury glow
A lantern by the waterfront
The soothing respire of the river;
I crossed a bridge to meet you
On the other side,
For the first time
All over again

And when the day is over
You carry me home,
Unfollowed
Though we are eclipsed.

I left a glass promise
On the steps of your monument
With the hope you will remember me
When I am older
And walls are only made of matter.

So rain me the colours of my country
Grow me green like the steep hills
And pavement cracks
And when it rains somewhere else,
I'll know the sound
As I have travelled there too.

Pte Edward George Cutt Two by Chris Bird

The Leaves fall,
Crustal and distant,
Our Past doesn't catch up,
The moment,
Like a glance,
Dissolves.

Eigengrau by Naino Masindet

"To err is human, to forgive, divine"
Absolve their sins, unshackle from one's own
Whilst every act remorseless by design
Will crown itself free will 'pon lawless throne.

His heart, the blotting with intrinsic light
The devil in his soul had twisted there,
He feels the cold more than a winter's plight
His conscience in repose with specious prayer.

If wayward machination's latest play
As much a magic trick mirror and smoke,
Must energy engaged in disarray
Transcribe as not his own to well provoke?

Forgive, but those of morose silhouette
Are not most immature to not forget.

Inmates by Tom Mallender

Confined behind walls
to hide from delicate view
the poor and sick.

Poverty hidden
poverty solved.

Small Hands by Naino Masindet

Clumsy and coarse
Like a restless mosaic,
Rough and tumble
Of white knuckled warfare --
Budding fists yearning
To bloom into open palms.

Small hands
Bound by soil and shackle,
Learn how to mend all
But what is broken
Dressed in jagged sunsets,
Pressed like a flower

The weight of the world for such

Small hands
With no love to hold
And the harbour
Now far behind them.

Dead Letter by Naino Masindet
(Inspired by "woman unknown")

Desolate page, crumpled and shredded by
Every iron hand. You still scrawl yourself to
Anyone who will listen. Now your consonants
Drag in viscous ink spills. You recall your
Language never being held to such ransom.
Emptied out on the cold stone, every
Trace of your foul undeserving, every plea spurned as
The retching of unholy mouth, condemned to
Erasure. This purgatory of retribution and
Remission houses no solace for a dead letter.

Being Rowdy Takes a Crowd by Tom Mallender

Anti-social behaviour
is generally a social activity.

It takes at least two to loiter.
Solo, you're just a lurker.

Loud, bolshie, lively or a nuisance,
it's always someone's judgment.

Alone you're just a…

Homesick by Naino Masindet

The heart is a missile
Guided by yearning
A currency of unrest
A raid for which there is no siren
No flash of light in the hallway
No clouds of sighs nor bones to dust
A whole world away from London
And yet, the explosion still found them.

Ten Days Leave by Naino Masindet
(Inspired by Jimmy Smith and Richard Blundell)

Medals of bravery garnished
beside a white cloth heart,
His fate to feast upon his chest

How could they have known the dawn
would always rise this way;
Lodged in the back of the throat

A morn they could nevermore
utter through even a
whiskey scented whisper.

And the rainfall condemns,
unrelenting
like a barrage of shellfire

sinking empty machines,
a sky's soft spoken word
in the poetry of battle.

Such is the sick and twisted spine
of war, how young men
surrendering their lives

Fall as martyrs of cowardice,
not a tower of strength
nor valiant heart.

For what is a man who could not keep
his word, for King and Country
forgiveness has no place.

What a way to get leave.

What a way to get leave.

*Private Jimmy Smith and Private Richard Blundell were friends who fought together in WWI, fighting at Passchendaele. Despite fighting in Gallipoli and the Somme and receiving two medals for good conduct, Smith was sentenced to death by firing squad for desertion. His friend Blundell was ordered to carry out the execution/ As a 'reward', the men of the firing squad were given ten days leave. Until his death in 1989, Blundell was haunted by these events, he was often heard murmuring, "What a way to get leave."

Poems by Post

A Scandal at School? by Tom Mallender

The school hummed
with hushed whispers.

One of the upper years found it,
or else commandeered it.

It, has an address on it.

It's, embossed in gold.

It's, somewhere in Irvine.

Two of the older girls
are going to write.

Enquire if there are more,
do they get one if they join?

Everyone wants it, or one just like it.

The headmaster hears reports of letters circulating.

He storms the classroom demanding the surrender
of rumoured correspondence.

Most likely,
the headmaster not expecting to receive
two letters of enquiry to the Irvine Poker Club
asking of pencils with painted sides.

Shining Like Spoken Gold by Chris Bird

The sudden colour
New, revitalising
A pencil to write down dreams
and summer days.
A child watching mice
join in at school.

The horizons of Scottish landscapes fade,
trains in the chill night.
Irish stars above deep blue seas
Her hands touch the window
of a rushing train,
she feels sure.

The beat of a train journey
from city to city
includes a life,
a hope,
flowering in the painted dusk.

Walked into Thought by Tom Mallender

The question?
Pos eisai
How are you?
Etsy ketsy,
The answer
So-so.

Nobby learned Greek in '44.
Was stationed there after the victory in the desert the year before.

From fighting across the periphery of civilisation's cradle to the birthplace of democracy and western philosophy.

Nobby remembers walking,
walking in Egypt,
walking in Palestine,
walking in Malta
then more walking in Greece.

Walking worked its way into Nobby's own philosophical creation
a companion motto to accompany
Etsy ketsy
a phrase still in use after 73 years:

"A lot of walking is the only way to get to places."

FEET (The March, 1945) by Mavis Pilbeam

I am just a pair of feet walking,
Left, right, left, right.
No mind for thought, no tongue for talking,
Left, right, left, right.
The cold has seized me, body and soul,
Frozen hard all sense of a goal,
Left   right

All consciousness, drained to my feet,
All else numb, dead beat.
Left   right

Those around me, scarecrows, ghosts,
Hounded by our grizzly hosts
Who scour the route for the next sign-posts:
Left
          Right

A place to fall and sleep the night;
Mouldy straw, no warmth, no light,
Soon roused again to our pitiless plight.
Left
          Right

Boots long gone, snow to the knee.

Villagers stand and stare, or flee.
This nightmare army who can they be,
Staggering, stumbling, drunkenly?
Left...

Another fallen, left to die:
No glance I spare him, no strength to cry,
To mutter a prayer, to say goodbye,
Just two feet walking — this is I.

Bruised, bloodied, raw to the bone,
Sickening sight! Shivering, I groan:
How can these ruined feet go on?

But on they must — or die alone.

            ...Right.

Mixed Feelings by Tom Mallender

Betty left school at 13,
to learn typing at a local Leeds college.

During the war Betty found herself
working at RAF Feltwell in Norfolk
secretary to the Commanding Officer
with the unenviable task
of writing to all the families
of those based at RAF Feltwell
who were lost.

At the time when his Majesty King George VI
visited Feltwell in May 1940
a Bomber Command crew member
had a worse chance of survival
than an infantry officer in World War One

Taking as an example
the statistical fate of 100 airmen:
55 were killed or died as a result of wounds.
14 were shot down;
12 of these were taken prisoner, often while wounded,
The other two were successful in evading capture.
Three were injured on operations or active service.

Leaving one to an uncertain fate and just 27
surviving to complete a tour of operations.
For most of the war an "operational tour",
consisted of 30 operations or flights.
This increased after D-Day
due to a perceived decrease in danger.

Sometime during 1945 orders came down
that it may be beneficial for some of the WAAF
to see the precision bombing sites.
The order was soon withdrawn.
But Betty,
having already been authorised to go,
joined the crew of a photo reconnaissance flight.

No other women stationed at
RAF Feltwell went,
thus Betty was the only one
to see what remained of Cologne
from the air in 1945.

She remembers wondering
"Where had the people gone?"

Betty still has very mixed feelings
about what she saw.

"The Germans had done the same to us
but it was very different to see."

Bell-Song by Mavis Pilbeam

Torrents of bell-song
clammer sky high
through cloud valleys,
springing from towers
where, tongues a-clatter,
ancient bells,
swing and poise,
ring and poise,
inevitably,
roped through pulleys,
down, down to cramped,
familiar rooms were,
balanced on boxes,
watching for rope sights,
inner eyes tracing routes
zigzag mid seas of maths,
the ringers pull, loose, pull, catch,
inevitably,
gladly unleashing
unseen overhead,
outpourings
through cloud valleys
clammering sky high,
torrents of bell-song.

Inventive by Tom Mallender

Bob at 84 and a half is one of the younger members
of this generation, perhaps one of the first teenagers
in the decade before they were invented.

Invention has had varying degrees of success
in Bob's life.

The joint discovery, shared with his friend
of removing the light bulb from a phone box
and to then loiter within range to offer chivalric
assistance, via a lighter
to any passing girls trying to use said phone box
in the pitch dark has paid off very well.

To date, Bob has 63 years and counting
of happy marriage attributed to that bit of
inventive thinking/minor vandalism.

Those serving under Bob's tutelage, have been
somewhat less stellar with their inventive
endeavors.

Fried eggs for breakfast,
garnished with the previous day's headlines
was the unique dining experience of 1953.
for the British Army of the Rhine.

Some bright spark, among the twenty
assigned to Bob thought they had devised of a plan
to save time, Cook the fried eggs for breakfast the
night before, leaving them on newspaper.

Thus, next morning, everyone was served eggs
with newspaper print on the back.

Dynasties, Eras and Legacies by Tom Mallender

East and West Hanney
are often referred to together, The Hanneys.

A slim field separates the two villages.
The field at its youngest must be a Saxon
but could be a Neolithic holdout.

The Hanneys is the place to live a long, long life.
There must be something in the waters
of Letcombe Brook, seeping through the villages.

The longest living Englishman,
in truth Englishwoman
Elizabeth Bowles lived in the villages.
She died in 1718.
She was born in 1594.

Elizabeth Bowles was born an Elizabethan,
witnessed the start and end of the Stuarts
spent time as a citizen of the commonwealth,
may well have celebrated both
the restoration
and then the glorious revolution
before dying a Georgian aged 124.

Visit the Hanneys today,
look in the Church on the north wall
there's a plaque to Elizabeth Bowles.

Forgotten by Chris Bird

Young thin faces become history,
their ordinary,
everyday bravery
becomes ordinary,
everyday sacrifice.

In fields lit by innocent sunshine,
they fell beside their shadows,
mouthing promises and other certainties,
they joined,
midnight armies.

Their young voices,
are silent now.

Prisoners, pilots,
boys,
heroes
the terms shift like metal name tags.

Their youth becomes a
fractured mask.
Their glances darken lonely horizons.

The sun breaking,
new shadows form,
soundlessly,
in streams of dutiful light.

My Part by Tom Mallender
(Inspired by Pat)

"I was young,
single and thought
I had better do my part"
Says Pat.

Looking around
at uniforms and duties,
she decided upon the
WAAF.

Seventy five years later,
with justified pride,
Pat still sports
part of that uniform.

She joined the WAAF,
apart from her appreciation of
the uniform,
as there would be no
undue amounts of
cooking, cleaning
mopping, polishing of floors
or washing.

Pat's service
took her far from her
home of Mile End
to the far reaches of Empire.

Part of doing her part
was flying.

Delivering planes which
could not be shipped in crates
or who's need was urgent.

RAF Third Tactical Air Force
were recipients of
Pat and her fellow WAAF
Pilots deliveries

She flew the Spitfires,
most likely assigned to
No. 224 Group RAF,
for use in operations
in support of
that forgotten14th Army
fighting in the Burmese jungle.

Pat says today:

"I was young
single
and thought
I had better do my part"

Stalag Luft III by Tom Mallender

What comes to mind?

An American on a motorbike?
A theme tune bleated out at a sports stadium?

Julie thinks of her brother,
Arthur.
An RAF airman shot down in 1942
after an operation over Malta
forcing it to ditch in the sea.

Only Arthur made it out,
carrying with him,
the final words of the pilot
to be conveyed to his wife.

The pilot and rest of the crew
were among the
two thousand three hundred and one
airmen killed or wounded
during the siege of Malta.

There Arthur was bobbing in the sea,
when a U-Boat broke the surface.
Kriegsmarine submariners came out onto deck.

" Ich kann Deutsch sprechen" Arthur hailed

Arthur was convinced
without his schoolboy German,
they would have left him to drown.

Taken ashore he was sent to Stalag Luft III.
The POW camp for allied aircrew.

Arthur soon joined one of the various escape
committees and set to work in the tunnels.

Conditions of camp life,
his injuries from being shot down
and the digging itself ravaged Arthur's health.
Leaving him unable to attempt escape.

This perhaps saved him from becoming murder
victim fifty-one of the Great Escape.

Near midnight, on January the 27th 1945,
when likely they could hear the Soviet advance,
only sixteen miles away
Arthur, along with eleven thousand other prisoners
were marched out at gun-point
from Stalag Luft III

Twenty-two thousand feet trudging through
shin deep snow soon drowned out
 the advancing Red Army.

On pain of death, they were marched 55 km.
before being given rest, then marched again.
Hundreds of prisoners were there put on trains.

Arthur and many thousands more were not.
They were marched to Stalag XIII-D.

Arthur arrived at an unknown date
where the Americans, truly enter Arthur's story
.
All prisoners at Stalag XIII-D
were marched, again at gun point
to Stalag VII-A which had been built
to hold 14,000 POWs.

In mid April 1945 it was holding over
130,000.
There Arthur was liberated on the 29th of April
1945
by the US 14th Armoured Division.

The Division forever after nicknamed the
Liberators.

An epitaph well-earned for liberators of;
Oflag XIII-B,
Stalag XIII- C,
Stalag VII-A,
and several of the sub-camps encircling
Dachau.

Freed Arthur was carried home
via the Red Cross,
both literally and figuratively.

Marched 500 miles through subzero temperatures
without shoes nor boots with snow to his shins
had all but destroyed Arthur's feet.

Julie remembers Arthur's return,
seeing her brother carried into the house.
A skeleton wearing a blue shirt.
Bandaged feet, stained and stinking,
perpetually ruined.

Julie chooses to remember Arthur as he was before
Stalag Luft III.

Lost Trades of Islington

Dolly by Tom Mallender

"I was born in Durham Road,
Finsbury Park in 1925."

Started nursery at four,
moved upstairs to Pools Park Primary School
at seven.
I left Hornsey Road school
at fourteen.

Went to the labour exchange,
shown round a factory near Essex Road.

"You start on Monday."

Ten shillings a week,
supplemented with piece work
with 2p taken off for insurance.
Woe betide you if you were late,
be docked sixpence.
Started at eight,
a tea break at your bench
then work until One.
An hour for lunch
then work until Five Thirty.

Used to walk to Finsbury Park Tube Station
to get to Essex Road.
After a while got a bike from a place in
Seven Sisters Road.

"Paid 2/6 to take it
then paid off the rest over time."

At the factory there were three floors.
The top floor made babies' napkins,
middle bandages and lint,
the other ladies' sanitary products.

Within 10 months of starting work
Dolly was taking home sixteen shillings a week.

Dolly became a charge hand of her specific bench
but didn't keep it long.

"Wasn't strict enough and figured you lost too
many friends as a charge hand
by telling them what to do too often.
I liked being friendly more than being in charge."

The factory employed around fifty people.
Each had a week's holiday a year plus Easter,
Whitsun and four days at Christmas.

"Out of the Christmas bag everyone would get a present from the manager and be treated to lunch."

"End of each week
I gave my wage packet to mum.
She'd give me a shilling out of it for spending."

Before the war Dolly would go dancing
or to one of the many cinemas.

"I would spend all my money while out.
We all did.
Used to walk home together
having spent our bus fare.

Mum's social life was to take a flask of tea down Hornsey Baths Laundry."

When the war broke out
Dolly wanted to join the land Army
but her dad said no.
She became an ARP Warden.

"Whenever the air raid sirens went I had to report for duty at Pools Park School when not at work. My Regular duty was to go round the houses ensuring there were no lights on.

Had to knock on doors to tell people that lights
were showing.
Wasn't very popular.
No [ARP] warden was!

The only training I had was civil defence training.
Put in a gas chamber where they gassed us.
I passed the test
just."

Dolly's most vital duty while in the Civil Defence
was to man the phones during an air-raid
informing the authorities where had been hit.

Everybody in the factory
had additional duties during the war
yet many did double shifts.

The medical supplies helped
bandage the frontlines.

Work in the factory carried during an air-raid.
Production stopping only when the bombing
reached a certain crescendo.
Only then could staff seek shelter
in the basement.

"The factory next door
was hit with a parachute bomb.
Both factories were abandoned
until they took it away.

Many nights when not on duty
spent down in Finsbury Park Tube Station."

Eunice by Tom Mallender

A beautiful bright dress shimmers,
In a Barbados dusk,
Soon in Brixton under new stars,
In a red brick street,
Factory scissors,
Cut and trim the days,
Of Clerkenwell.

Women's Work by Phoebe Smith

The opaque sheet covers the surface like a cataract
as I
    trace
        draw
            copy
                follow
                    the proscribed lines.

I allow myself to saunter peacefully
through this maze of ordered complexity,
admiring the confident angles and perfect arcs,
smiling at the interlocked parallels
anchored with self-assured junctions.

I relish the careful replication,
of powerful signs and hieroglyphs,
never doubting their ability to provide an answer.
To me, the uninitiated, they remain a mystery.

Lately I have started to notice the hesitations,
the insecurities.
Perhaps the slightly imperfect circle
or the light feathering where wet ink
has brushed against the rule.
This I find disturbing.

I have begun to add my own healing components.
Sometimes a tiny little terrapin,
nestling in the date stamp
or the flourish of a signature
containing the perfect Norwegian coastline.
Today it was a beautiful set of cutlery,
tucked away in the margin, barely visible.

Why by Phoebe Smith

was sixpence a tanner
two shillings, a two bob bit
two shillings and sixpence
a half crown,
three pennies,
a thrupenny'bit.
a pound was a quid
a penny a copper.

And all by the end of the day
made
your hands
smell all funny

Evacuation by Phoebe Smith

Time doesn't heal
it simply passes.
She still cries at the brutality,
the unexplained nastiness,
inflicted by strangers
upon
such a frightened little girl.

the story of most
is not the story
of all.

Evacuated aged six,
returned aged eighteen,
she loved her country life.
Elective affection
for a different growing,
one she didn't want to leave,
ever.

the story of most
is not the story
of all.

Initiation by Phoebe Smith

after six years
you think ' I don't go in that day'
but they'd come round your house
and get you,
to make sure . . .

they'd strip you
and put you in a barrow,
with flour, water and tomato ketchup
all different things you have on the table,
they'd soak you in it.
push you down to old street,
and you'd come back nude,
all the way.

no showers in them days,
just buckets of cold water,
really cold.

That's it,
you was skilled.

Coach Building by Phoebe Smith

More than a lost trade, more than a lost skill,
it's a lost language.
Trailers used to come in flat
twenty four feet long,
two blokes to each trailer,
three weeks to build from new.
Everything all wood,
hand tools and chisels.
Big cutting, like roof sticks and standards
was cut on band saws,
standards what hold the panels on,
then roof sticks, camp roll,
put on the matching,
tack down the roof sheet on the sticks,
paint it before the moldings went on,
two or three coats, then a sealer.
Three weeks,
from new.

Cakes by Post, 1902 by Angela Bailey

A four-page leaflet
printed at considerable expense,
a hundred Beale's cakes
illustrated in colour,
one inserted into every copy
of The Strand Magazine.

Orders poured in from all parts
of the country,
from abroad as well,
tropical countries included.
A ridiculous idea!

The dispatch department had only
greaseproof paper, wood shavings,
cardboard boxes and string
for sending cakes
by His Majesty's parcel post.

I shudder to think
of the condition of our cakes
arriving in summertime
at Calcutta or Hong Kong.

Trade dropped off

as quickly as it had started;
happily no deaths were reported
at home or abroad.
The scheme was William's last
"folie de grandeur".

Beale's Store, Holloway: Fraternal Disputes
by Angela Bailey

On the thirteenth day
of the month
the board of directors met
to authorise payments.

William the First
signed all the cheque
unable to trust his sons
and the company secretary
not to run off with the cash
the minute his back was turned.

Annual profit and loss accounts
for each department -
right down to the last halfpenny -
led to fraternal fighting,
each believed his departments,
his alone,
kept the company from bankruptcy.

The nineteenth century
drew to a close.
the long reign of William the First*,
like that of Queen Victoria,
did not long survive it.

Let's Write Hammersmith and Fulham 2023

McDonald's by Freeman

I eat chips, chips, chips and more chips. I really want to drink the Grimace Shake because people say it tastes good. I like to eat ice cream.

Adventures in London by Adnan

Once upon a time, there was a girl called Naya and a boy called Adnan. They liked adventures and they wanted to go and then they saw a treasure hunt and wanted to play. They played and they won and they really wanted to go and eat. Soon they helped their dad to clean up the house, they were exhausted from cleaning. After, they went to sleep and they wanted to hear a bedtime story and then they went to sleep. One day they were dreaming of going to a fun day in their dreams. They woke up with no energy and they didn't want to do cleaning.
The End

Magic Carpet Story by Rameen

Today I invented a device that makes it possible to talk to animals. It is a carpet and if you roll it on the floor and place an animal on it, it can talk like a human. I brought 100 cats, 100 horses, 100 dogs and 100 turtles. I rolled the carpet on the floor and placed all the animals on the carpet.
All of a sudden I heard several shouts and screams. I heard, "OH NO WE GOT CAPTURED BY THAT HORRIBLE HUMAN!" I was baffled. "I'm not a horrible human!" I screamed. After I said that there was silence. All the animals stared at me with wonder. "Did she just talk?" asked a horse named Betty. "I think so?" whispered a cat called Emily. "Okay just understand this. The carpet under you is magical." I explained. "AAAA!" they screamed. Very soon after they screamed I heard a knock. *Oh no it might be my nosy neighbour,* I thought. I quickly rolled the carpet with the animals still in there. I put on loud music to cover the muffled sounds. I opened the door. I was right, it was my nosy neighbour. "I thought I thought I heard some sounds," she said.

Jolof by Voita

Jolof is a football club in Sands End. There is a lot of people there.
Fun Facts:
Jolof wins a lot of tournaments for example they won one that was 5-0.
They won over one hundred cups!
It is the best team in England!
You will never see an own goal, a open goal miss or even a corner in embarrassing moments!
Jolof hardly loses, they only lose when they are not playing their best but they score every match.
The End
(Jolof is the best)

The Adventure at Pineapple Park by Aya

Once upon a time there was a girl called Sofia. She was going to Pineapple Park every day after school. She was going to Pineapple Park then she found an Adventures castle! She went in it! People were there, she made so many friends! "Wow I have so many friends!" exclaimed Sofia. Finally she found a treasure chest. Thank you friends, thank you very much for being my friends.

A Fun Time at South Park by Ralph

One day I was wandering around in South Park with my friends. When we found a clear space we set down a picnic. Next we set down two goals to play football and we made a huge football tournament and whoever won could pick 5 people to go to a huge party. And whoever lost would still have a fun time there. There were 4 teams which were the Huge Ice Blocks, the Burning Wolves, the Fantastic Ballers and the Ferocious Bears.
When it started it was the Fantastic Ballers and the Huge Ice Blocks. At the end it was 2-1 for the Fantastic Ballers. Then the Burning Wolves were against the Ferocious Bears and it was 0-0 at the end. The finals were intense and it was 5-5 and they both had a fun party while the others had a fun little picnic.

Two Snippets by Sumaiyah, Intisar

In gymnastics I compete with my teammates and I sometimes win a gold medal and I feel proud. When I'm on stage I feel nervous and happy at the same time.

What if... you had a cat and when you were cooking it jumped at you and burnt you so badly you went to the hospital and broke your leg and arm.

The Two Best Friends by Adelaide

One day when Adelaide was at her gymnastics she found a girl called Alice. Her and Adelaide immediately became friends for they both bonded over much. After gymnastics the two new friends played adventures at the South Park. They loved exploring through the bushes. Although it was time to go after long. Alice and Adelaide still are great friends.

Then they were doing one of their adventures, they got surrounded by snakes! So they quickly hopped on helicopters and flew to Australia. There they fell asleep upside down with the bats. After they smushed leaves to get clean water and ate some carrots they found on a hill but it was hard to get the carrots for the mountain was very steep so they asked a goat to take them up in exchange for some of the carrots. They found the goat but they had to cross a lava pit so they swung across vines to rescue the goat and get the carrots. Wait till next time to see what adventures happen next!

Another Again by Alisa

Once at South Park there was a lost cat that didn't like having fur. The cat was never born because one day she just appeared out of nowhere!
Then one day another cat came by and also didn't have any owner. Then the cat saw the other cat and just remembered that exactly the same thing has happened before. But then the other cat went to her and asked her name. She didn't really know what to say so she said her nickname. So she said that her name was Allie. Then the other cat said her name. The other cat said that her name was Lilly.

Lilly followed Allie everywhere but then one day Allie noticed that but Lilly kept doing it, it got a bit nerve-racking for Allie. So one day Allie stood up for herself and said, "Stop following me Lilly." So then Lilly stopped doing that and Allie found herself a new friend.

A Magic Place by Lina

One day, a girl called Rima was eating her special breakfast because... it was her birthday. Normally each year her parents bring her to Fulham library and can get as many books as she could but this year it was different.

Normally she recognised a path to the library. "What's this place?" asked Rima to her parents. SURPRISE! The room was all dark with loads of bright lights, the walls were formed differently. It was a climbing place. Rima was really shy, she doesn't know how to climb.

Just then, a woman with beautiful dark hair with wide eyes came straight to the family. "Hello!" said the woman, "my name is Sandi. You are going to explore the Clip 'n Climb Centre." "But I don't know how to climb!" "That's why we are here to help!"

Happiness by Angeline

Walking up Bloemfontein Road, the cool wind keeps pulling me back making my jacket left up in the air like Batman's cape. I keep walking forward. I should speed up because I am late for my sessions.
Will the water be cold today? Oh, whatever! Let me just cannonball into the deep end!
I'm cold! I'm freezing! I need to get out!... Oh, wait… I'm not cold anymore. It's time to have some fun!
All around me the glittering water is pulsing up and down. The children are joyfully splashing as if they were bouncing on a trampoline. Others are jumping about like dolphins diving in the ocean.
"Hey, Mum, look at me!"
It's time to do some flips, handstands and cartwheels. Next, I will glide under all the swimmers. I'm getting better at holding my breath. 15 minutes to go! I'd better do some races and laps with my mum before time runs out.
I love coming to the Janet Adegoke Swimming Centre. I can't wait to come back!

The End by Albane

A gnome popped out the drain.
"Hello" Miranda said, "is it Poppy, Sage or Ale?"
"Neither" said the gnome, "I'm parched!"
"Oh, hello Parched!" said Mimi.
"No, I am parched," explained the gnome.
"Yes, I know, you told me!" persisted Mimi.
"Can I have some water now?" asked the exasperated gnome.
"Sure Parched!" replied Miranda.
"For the last time, I was parched, then you gave me water, I am no longer parched and my name has always been Petal!" said the gnome.
"Oh," said Mimi, "so sorry!"
She brought Rose into the kitchen and made some tea and biscuits.
"I hope your journey here from Unmatched was alright?" asked Mimi.
"Well, you know they have installed a new entrance on the Golden Gate Bridge so it was much quicker!" exclaimed Petal, "My friend should be here soon."
"Is he parched?" inquired Mimi.
"Yes, how did you know, in fact his whole name is Parched the III!" he squealed.
"Oh" replied Mimi.

Marketplace by Zoya

Piles of passionfruit
Mangoes galore
Handfuls of berries
Want some more?
The whiffs of spices
The feel of cool wind
They lower the prices
as I walk in
I taste a French pastry
Slurp down my peach tea
Find anything the heart desires
at the market of your dreams

Dragons Are Real by Oscar

Many moons ago there was a city in Roma. Roma was very rich but there was one problem. A rich man's home was getting took over by a dragon! Every night you can hear him snoring from miles away. The rich man had to do something about it so he went to the witch's hut.
When he arrived, he asked for a potion. The witch chose a random one. He turned into a …. Lion. He got back home and waited until night, but the dragon wasn't there. He looked around but no one was there. He waited for the next night and the dragon was there. He ate the dragon and the dragon was defeated.
                    The END
                    or is it…?

"What if a koala went on an adventure?"
by Cienna, Nadia

It would wear a hat, an adventure suit and exploring glasses. It would go exploring in the forest and have a great, amazing day. The koala will see a spider, slugs, snakes and other creatures. It would sleep on long trees have food when this man comes every day and knows where to go. And travels the world after.

He will probably go on an airplane. He will probably sleep the whole time but let's see what he is up to. He's eaten and slept, went to the toilet, tried to escape, escaped went to the captain and released all the animals, went to the captain again and the plane crashed.

What Is a Griffin? by Sofia

A rustle from the bush
It soon set fire
A flap of its wings
A mean desire.
A screech, two more
Filled the air
Not a wolf, not a bear …
Who what where?
A tail whipped me
My eyes are closed
A fire crackled, so hot, so crispy
It would burn my toast.
I opened my eyes
Panicked and afraid.
A beak, two eyes
I fell back in surprise.

Oldilocks by Nadia

A witch once turned Goldilocks into an old person so her friends called her Oldilocks instead of Goldilocks. It was really hard for her to wake up but she made it home. The three bears were stunned but now baby bear couldn't play with Oldilocks.
After a week Oldilocks was back to Goldilocks so baby bear and Goldilocks can play again.
Goldilocks told them what happened and then they told the police. So the witch was sent to prison.

Mysterious Box – Vegetables by Alessandra

A mysterious box appeared in town 2 days ago. Nobody knows what's inside, they can't get it open. Since its arrival half the town has grown vegetables on their heads. This morning, my headteacher came into school with a carrot sprouting out of her head and all the English teachers had broccoli on theirs. Bill had a beetroot on his.
Nobody can prise open the box and stop the curse of overgrown spuds on my aunt's head. Perhaps it's a good thing. I can definitely get used to having cucumbers whenever I'm feeling peckish!
Actually, never mind. I'm only an hour into having cucumbers on my head that I'm really craving something else… Perhaps the parsnips on the mayor's head?

"What if you were able to play your sport for your favourite sports team?" by Cienna, Linda

I like playing football because it's fun and I like the team sport because most of my friends play with me. Also, I got really good at it because in our school we have a football pitch and even though I don't practice a lot in school and playcentre I still love it.

What if I got to play on my favourite gymnastics team. It would be a dream come true. What if it was on the moon, I could fly high while doing flips but can it become true it would be a dream if I got to play on my favourite gymnastics team on the moon.

Light by Albane

The wind and the moon,
together made whole.
I see the cluster,
the crags and the holes.
The light is not scars
not dark but not light.
I see a large owl,
strong and in flight.
I often wonder,
when the people will see
How much beauty,
there is to be seen.
So open your eyes,
let some light in,
and tell yourself,
that beauty is no sin.

The Unknown Power by Oscar

Once many moons ago, there was a young boy called Jake. Jake was playing basketball and he noticed he was bouncing the ball high. He played tennis and hit it miles up in the sky. He now knew his secrets, he had SUPERPOWERS!
He did other tests and they didn't work. Jake went to school and got angered by the bully and fire burst out his mouth. He knew straight away he had more superpowers. He could cook food in less than a minute, but... he could only use it when he is mad. Jake got home and heard his mum say that he is going to a roller coaster ride. He was so cheerful he got outside and jumped around while he was jumping, he started to lift up. He could fly but only when he is excited.
Jake could hit hard normally, breathe out fire when he's angry and fly when he's excited. What's next? Sadness? Worried?
It's up to you …

Lost in a Forest by Henry

So, first he arrived in the first forest. Who knew what was in that forest? Maybe an army of Zombies!
He rapidly made his way through the first half of the forest. Where he came to a wide opening. He stopped to have a breath, SUDDENLY! A big large monster popped out. In a deep dark voice, the monster said
"I am known as…"

Love by Albane

If someone loves you far and near
it will break a mountain.
If love is strong and sound
then no obstacle will bar it.
For if you love and if you're loved
then nothing will stand in your way.

Short Story by Alessandra

"And this is how the Egyptians were one of the most impressive civilizations in the whole history of the Earth" concludes my incredibly boring history teacher. It was just another ordinary history lesson until my father burst into the classroom, grabs me by the ear and tells me that we need to leave town in an hour. He then grabs me outside, bundles my brother and I into our old, run-down Audi and drives my family off at top-speed.

After at least 20 minutes of stunned silence, my father announced what this was all really about: at the lab in which he works in, it was prophesised that a monsoon of poisonous, acid rain was going to befall us all very, very soon. After hours, or perhaps even days, we arrived into a very dark and deep forest in which we trekked for hours until, deep underground, there was a small bunker. It had all we needed to survive for the years during the monsoon.

All of a sudden, I heard it. The rain had begun. At first, it was nothing more than a gentle tapping against the roof of the bunker but then it became a stronger, faster tapping which rapidly evolved into a full-blown rainstorm. It raged for many days until we ran out of food. My mother put on a special rain-suit to protect her from the rain. A few days and we took turns until one day, my mother went out and accidently left the door slightly open. The rain streamed in. Using her instincts, she tried to use the sleeve of her raincoat to close it up. However, the concentration of rain was now too potent. She had gotten wet; I never saw my mother again. Life in the bunker then became dismal and dark. Although she had saved our lives hers had gone.

After a few days, we wondered if we would ever feel the warmth of the sun or at least a day without the tapping of the rain. The rain that could end all of humanity.

Months later, we began to notice that the rain was not so loud and strong. We even at times could not hear the rain at all. Slowly, we relaxed and even went out a few times without our rainsuits! However, it was a false alarm. My father had gone out to a meeting with the other survivors when the rain began once again. Perhaps he survived.

Days later, my brother and I discover a toolbox in which you could contact other bunkers. No one reacted or replied to mine or my brother's cries and pleas for help. So, we waited. We got on with our ordinary lives whilst the rain keeps tapping and tapping. I wonder if it will ever stop. Perhaps it could, sometime in the future. In the meantime, the rain taps on the bunker roof.

The Moon by Zoya

The Moon
It orbits us.
It shines and provides a glow in the night,
The moon.
It's our sense of night and day
The stars
They are similar to the moon
They twinkle
The lake
It holds a reflection
A box of some sort
This box holds a key
this box holds the moon

Poem by Alessandra

A single tree stands on a mountain.
Its gnarled branches interweaving.
Years of strong winds have taken its toll,
the tree slowly bends lower and lower.
Alone on a mountain,
surrounded by stone.
A sprout of life appears,
contrasting to the grey sky.

The Cave of Mankind's Secrets
by Thomas and Nolan

In the ancient times of mankind there was a mysterious cave called Elude cave.... There were many theories stored in an abandoned chest in an unknown place in Elude cave. This was since the beginning of time.
In 400AD, there were 2 boys who lived in Gasalonia who tried to find Elude cave. Their mum was from Hitaly and their dad died of cancer. Their mum would only let them go to the supermarket when she was grocery shopping.
After, the boys paced up and down to think of a plan. They would escape, so they had to pack up orange juice, cheesy toes and a torch. The plan was to bribe the cops to arrest the mother for kidnapping.
As they set on their journey, they glanced at the fragile map. They realised that they had to hire a boat to cross the Pacific Ocean. So, they visited a friend called Thomlan who had lots of boats. When they got there, they asked how many bitcoins to purchase the mother boat, he said 6 bitcoins. The boys agreed and paid but there's a catch which is that the Pacific Ocean had an unknown species...

In the middle of the Pacific they crashed and then KO'd. When they woke up, they saw the Elude Cave and the chest of many theories that were answered…

They saw many booby traps like poisoned darts and maces. They were SHOCKED!!! But in the meantime, one of the boys was hit by a dart and died. When they made it to the chest the boys died as the other one saw something special inside the chest but the unknown had awoken.

Samurai Ninjas by Junaid

Introduction

Once upon a time there lived a world of Ninjas until the Snake Master used a spell so powerful, he couldn't control it and Samurai and Ninjas were mixed and now Master Kick is training 3 Samurai Ninja called Bolt, Kia and Tommy. These Samurai Ninjas are going to unleash their full potential and defeat the Time Snake Monster.

Chapter 1 - The Show Off

"Watch this Kia I can control the lights," said Bolt.
"That's just a show off, but this is not" replied Kai.
"If that's not then controlling lights isn't," said Bolt.
"But look at this I can do both" said Tommy.
"That's not fair" said Kai and Bolt.
"Stop showing off and get rest" said Master Kick.

Chapter 2 – No Tomorrow

The next day or should I say, the same day. After a while Kai, Bolt and Tommy realised it was the same day straight away. They knew it was the Time Snake Monster and tracked him down.

Chapter 3 – The Captive Slips Through
As soon as they found him, they took him to the dungeon. After a while he used a spell and slipped through the bars.
Where could he have vanished?

Sands End Adventures in Creativity

Samurai Ninjas 2: Don't Miss by Junaid

Wondering
While Kai, Bolt and Tommy were in PE they were still puzzled about where the time snake master was. Suddenly, they were hit by a dodgeball. Frantically, their PE teacher shouted "on the bench".

Gaming
Later that day, they started playing FC24. They were bored so they started playing Fortnite. They still wondered where the time snake monster was. They tried locating any magic. Suddenly, they were teleported into Fortnite!

Teleported
Suddenly, they heard a voice. The voice said "kill 80 people in Fortnite. Retrieve a green emerald which grants you your powers which are the sting of a scorpion, the climbing of a tiger, the bite of a crocodile and the speed of a cheetah."

Starting
They pressed a start button. When they started they were hit. A computer above them said you lost against the S Twins. They searched for people to kill. They found a letter that said 'you are invited'. They went there and killed them. The computer said only ten more people.

Almost Done
They got a hint. The hint said "high where you fly is where you will find the key to ride." They thought. Kai said, "the only thing that flies is the battle bus!" Kai always figures everything out. Anyways, where were we. Tommy says "but how will we get there?" Bolt started to look around. He said "guys, I have an idea, what if we build a staircase to the battle bus." Kai and Tommy thought it was a great idea.

The Idea Worked
They started to build. When they finished the battle bus wasn't there so they had to wait 30 minutes. Finally, it arrived. They climbed up the staircase and found 10 people and had shot them and won. They got sent to a black room. Suddenly they heard a voice say "you won congratulations, you have gained your powers. The sting of a scorpion, the speed of a cheetah, the climbing of a tiger and the bite of a crocodile."

Back Home
They were teleported back home. It was the next day and they were late for school. Bolt had a suggestion, "How about I piggyback you with my super speed to school."

Bloom Quist by Olivia and Stefy

Once upon a time there lived a girl named Stefy. She travelled the world with her mother Leila Thristledown (she was a journalist) but one day they were sitting in a café near Kew Gardens when her ma told her that she was gonna go to the Amazon rainforest. But then her ma said that she had to go to boarding school and handed her a device and said this will keep you safe if anything happens. Then her mother drove her to Gelston, a girl boarding school at the countryside. After she led her to the principal on the way she saw a girl staring at her in the corridor. She was about to go and talk to her when she was pushed into the principal's office and her ma left her. After some pep talk with the principal, she tried to find the girl who was staring at her in the hallway but she couldn't find her so she headed over to the cafeteria. She saw the girl sitting in a seat by the corner eating pasta. So she headed over to her then the girl opened her school bag and started talking to it. Stefy thought this was very weird so she started spying on the girl. Soon after Stefy got a ridiculous idea that Olivia's bag was alive. The girl spotted Stefy and blushed. Stefy did the same. That's when they noticed they looked quite alike.

And that's when they had a big memory shift and realised they were sisters. Suddenly the bag fell down and a squirrel jumped out!

Stefy started screaming while Olivia held the squirrel back. Then Olivia started talking to the squirrel in a weird language and the squirrel stopped fighting. Then Olivia dragged Stefy to the girls' toilet and locked the door and started explaining herself in detail. "I'm so sorry, I didn't want to tell you we were sisters and about the squirrel." Then Olivia started apologising at the same time. Then Stefy had a flashback in her memory again, she remembered that Olivia was 1 minute younger than Stefy and that a flu came into her town and killed her parents and Olivia and Stefy were separated. They hugged each other and Stefy made Olivia promise never to keep secrets again.

Cat and Dolphin by Maya

The cat and dolphin
Swimming in the sea
Drinking boba
Juicily

Untitled by Rosalie

Once upon a time lived a Youtuber called Robby. The channel was called Robby and Penny, Penny was one of his dogs but he has two.
But his house was haunted every night he heard footsteps coming from the door with the basement in it.
The twist was his dogs were always with him. So he recorded a video with his ring camera. Then he poured flour on the floor. In the morning he got up and saw footsteps. He checked the cameras. He saw footsteps walking but there was no one. He had enough he went into the room and opened the basement. He left after he found a doll.

Untitled by Nadia

Once there was a little boy named Alan. Alan loved playing football but he was only 6 years old. His favourite football team was Real Madrid.
One day, Alan was playing football he kicked the ball over the fence. So, he went to get it when he was there he saw dun dun dun… a tiny gingerbread house. "How could that get there." Alan's eyed widened with shock.
Alan saw a mail box with gingerbread women and a gingerbread men. He silently chose the gingerbread men and ate it. "Why's the ball getting bigger?" He asked himself. "Ahh I'm too small!" Now his voice was squeaky like a mouse's. He didn't care about football anymore but his coach was calling him. He didn't care so he entered the mysterious house. "Wow this is amazing." He saw…… a gingerbread world! First he saw a gingerbread house. Then he looked around him and saw thousands of gingerbread people in a gingerbread market. He thought this was a dream.

Finch by Olivia

Finches oh so energetic
With red bellies like Mars.
Their chirping is so nice,
Just like paradise.
What a shame that cats steal their fame.

Welcome to Space by Lina

"I'm so excited!" shouted Ben. His parents said yes to go to space. And he just finished his spaceship to go to space! His mum just finished the space costume. Now, Ben was sitting in his spaceship prepared to go to space. He pressed a button and whoosh flew through the air. "Yeee!" shouted Ben. 2 minutes later, Ben could see stars in the sky: he was approaching space. It was a marvellous sight. He could see Mars, Jupiter, the moon and even the earth just behind him. He really wanted to do this because his teacher gave him lots of information about space. So, he wanted to find out more about space. The ship landed with a CRASH on Mars, Ben didn't panic because he went on rollercoasters a lot. He got out of the space ship and took pictures. "Yoohoo!" shouted Ben. He shouted because he was flying because of gravity. He flew to the moon and saw aliens. "Boo ba la!" they said, "Oh hello," replied Ben. The aliens gave Ben a diamond and he thanked them. Ben got back to the earth and showed the sparkly diamond to his parents. Ben went to sleep and dreamed about the aliens he saw in space.

Fortnite by Vivan

1. Welcome
Hello new player. Welcome to Fortnite. I will guide you to victory!

2. AOG
As you might have seen in trailers you all might have to kill, but not your team. You have to build a lot to make your opponents scared and keep close to your team.

3. Playing
You will have to jump out of the battle bus and go to a non-famous place like the forest and then farm for mats. Mats means materials. After that go to Snooty Steppes and kill Peter Griffin to get his shotgun and medallion. A medallion is a coin that heals you up (by shield).

4. Winning
Great job only person left. You will get into a build fight 1v1. Once you win you get a victory crown. Top tip. YOU COULD GET V-BUCKS TO BUY SKINS

The Kind Heart by Maya

Once at night there was a little girl snoring looking tired. But then she heard a little twinkle outside so she woke up looked out the window and guess what she found! She found a heart flying through the sky but she thought she was losing her mind so she just went back to sleep. The next morning she woke up and she had the best day ever. The heart's job was to go across the world to spread happiness and joy. Because the heart had one power and it was whenever she went next to somebody they get happiness and joy. On and on people were getting happy. But she never know how it felt to be happy and one day she found two animals one was a red panda and the other was a cat they looked like this: Those animals were amazing. Every day she went to those animals which she called friends. One day she suddenly felt what joy meant so the heart thanked her friends for finally showing the meaning of happiness. She happily had the best life ever playing with her friends and spreading joy.

Rocks of Fortune by Rosalie

Amethyst purple light
Topaz shining bright
Aquamarine read for flight

Mrs Meow's Adventure by Lina

Once there was a white and grey cat that lived in London called Mrs Meow. She lived in a little house. It was 1:00 in the afternoon. Mrs Meow was searching on Youtube how to cook fish and chips. "I'm so hungry!" Mrs Meow thought. She put the chips in the oven and the fish in the second oven she had. She went to the living room. "I wonder if I could take holidays," she wondered. She turned the TV on. "The marvellous Cirque du Soleil is opening tomorrow for 2 months. It is the best show ever." The cat with a tie said in the TV.

Suddenly, Mrs Meow's eyes brightened. "I know! I will go to Cirque du Soleil." After she reserved a seat for the show, a beep came up to her ear. "Ah! The supper is finally ready!" She ran to the oven and opened it. "Yum!" she said. She placed the chips and fish on a plate and started eating. When she finished, she went upstairs to her room to read more about the show. "Beautiful pictures!" she said. 3 minutes later, she called her friend, Maya. "I'm going to Cirque du Soleil!" Mrs Meow said. "So lucky!" Maya replied. "She we meet in McDonald's?" Maya asked. "Sure!" Mrs Meow replied.

Night time came and Mrs Meow was designing dresses, Mrs Meow took her phone and typed *should we meet now?* "Sure" Maya typed back. McDonald's was next to Mrs Meow's house so she went downstairs, took her coat and got outside. The sky was dark blue and Mrs Meow was shivering. *I should have brought a scarf,* she thought. When she arrived, she saw Maya and both of them went inside. "I already ordered what I want: a strawberry milkshake and a chicken burger," she replied. "Well, I will just take a vanilla milkshake," Mrs Meow said. While they waited, Mrs Meow showed loads of photos of Cirque du Soleil. "It's beautiful, I am definitely gonna reserve," Maya said. "Can you sit next to me?" Mrs Meow asked, "In the 14th row?" While Maya reserved, Mrs Meow walked to the counter to collect the food. When they finished eating, both of them walked back home.

Normally, Mrs Meow sleeps at midnight so she wasn't tired. She went upstairs to get changed into her pyjamas and went downstairs to watch TV. 3 hours later, Mrs Meow got to bed. She was so excited about tomorrow she couldn't even sleep!

When she woke up the next morning, Mrs Meow walked downstairs to her garden to breathe some fresh air. She got inside to prepare her breakfast: toast and fish. She remembered she will be meeting Maya at the Royal Albert Hall for the show at 10:30. So she quickly ate and went upstairs to change. Then she got back down, took her backpack and put snacks inside.

When she got out the house she walked past the postcat, Mr Addinson. She said hello and went to the train station. Luckily the train Mrs Meow took directly came. When she went inside, she put on her headphones and listened to music. After passing four stations Mrs Meow got off the train. She ran up the stairs. She was about to run again, but then she saw Sainsbury's, they gave the best fish crisps ever. Mrs Meow's eyes sparkled. She did not have that snack in her bag. "I'm definitely going there," she said and ran to the shop.
After stashing the crisps inside her bag, Mrs Meow ran and followed the map. When the map said Mrs Meow was finally here, Mrs Meow moved her head up. A big magnificent sphere was just in front of her, she was there. A big statue of a cat was placed in front of the sphere. Mrs Meow took a picture with her camera and walked to the door where

Maya was waiting. "I'm so excited" they both said. When a cat police opened the door for them Maya checked the map. "We have to go through 3 levels," Maya said. "Let's use the elevator," Mrs Meow replied. When they got in the 4th floor Maya asked a cat where was the theatre and the man pointed at an opened door. Maya and Mrs Meow walked to the door. The theatre was gigantic. It was really dark inside. When Maya and Mrs Meow took their seats, a cat appeared and done cool flips. The show started. After 2 hours of amazement, Mrs Meow and Maya said goodbye to each other to go to their houses.

The Pirate Made of Cheese who Lives in McDonald's by Rosalie

The pirate was eating cheeseburgers then he turned into cheese!? "What the barnacles, I'm yellow ooh ah de do do oh no I'm being eaten what the nitrogen dioxide" he was never to be eaten, I mean, seen again.

KFC by Bonnie and Faith

Whenever you're hungry, never hesitate to ask your parents to eat KFC.

The Girl and The Ghost by Nadia

There once lived a girl that believed in ghosts and had lots of mirrors because she saw a myth that if you put five mirrors facing each other the ghost will come to you. She used a luigi board every day to see if she could make another friend. But one day she tried to get another mirror and… she finally got a new friend! She put on her ghost glasses and she found the ghost on her bed so she found out it was her great grandad that died in world war 2. She went to her bed and used her ghost voice. She knows that that's her granddad because she knew that her great granddad always wore the necklace that her mom gave to him for his birthday. Sadly, after 2 months after his birthday he passed away. They buried him under their house. It turned out that the girl's name was ghostly. That's why she loved loved loved ghosts and even used ghost technology every day.

C.A.T Meme War by Malia and Max

Chapter 1: An Unexpected Guest
On an island far and distant, there's a secret society called "C.A.T memes." C.A.T stands for Cute And Terrifying. These have many stupid places all over the world. Like out in the open which says "C.A.T" on top of it. Maybe it's in someone's basement they didn't even know about. However, one faithful night an anonymous creature enters the main lair. SLAM! The door crashed open. The cold chill froze the inside. A creature who seemed to be a NON-CAT meme appeared in the middle of the room. The opening door shows the rainy outside world. Every meme in the room hissed in fear and the unknown creature walked in. "I have come to speak to your master, Happy Cat."
"I will never tell you Banana Cat's location."
"Fine. I will just have to find him myself," the creature said.
"HA! As if you'll find his secret compartment called 'Banana basement'."
"Wait, what did you…"
"NOTHING!"
"HEY!!" said an unknown voice. "What's going on here?"

"I don't know!!" Happy Cat shouted, "But **HE** came and destroyed everything by coming here!"
"Who are you exactly?!" said the unknown voice.
"I," said the creature, "I am Toothless dancing meme."

Chapter 2: Apple and Bananas
"Ha, as if I would believe you're the one the only Toothless dancing meme," the voice said, "The one that blew up the internet?"
"Yep!" he said proudly.
"Cap!" the voice said.
"Well, who are you then?" Toothless said.
"I am Banana Cat's DEPUTY," it said, "Apple Cat!"
"Yeah, yeah, yeah. You're **SO** special." Happy Cat said wryly.
"Apple Cat!" a voice came from the intercom.
"Come to my office this instant! And make sure the visitor comes to see me." it said. "We need to talk."

LATER:
"So, you're the guy hosting this whole society. Huh," Toothless said, "Pretty short for a… leader."
"APPLE CAT. As deputy you should know, greeting our guests and bringing them to ME to discuss further investigation!" Banana Cat said.
"Or what!?" Apple Cat said.

"Or. You'll become another treat for the outside RAIN!!!"
"Sorry b...boss." Apple Cat said in fear.
"You," Banana Cat said, "you must be that Toothless dancing meme which is on the internet."
"And you must be the famous Banana Cat, aren't you?" Toothless said.
"Yes." He said, "so what brings you here on this terrifying night. Are you cold? Are you hungry, thirsty. Here let me get you some tea or…"
"I need to talk about the war that's been going on between C.A.T memes and the other memes!"
"Oh," Banana Cat said shocked, "that's why you're here."

Chapter 3: Smurf Cat?!
SLAM! Slam! Slam!
"Uh, I'm here to register for uh…" said a voice behind the door.
"You're 10 minutes late!" Apple Cat exclaimed through the camera.
"WHAT?! HOW!" the voice said in shock.
"Jk" Apple Cat laughed.
"Oh, whelp, I am…" it said.
"So what's the harm, kid," the camera interrupted.
"I was going to say my name was…"
"Oh you can just tell me on the way," the camera

said, "Walk and talk?"
"K."

A BIT LATER:
"Follow me" camera said. "And you will see how sophisticated this place truly is."
"By the way my name is…"
"Nobody ASKED!" camera shouted in anger. "So what meme are you?"
"Oh. I'm not a meme, more like the creatures who take care of the cats around here." He said proudly.
"So. What's your name?"
I… I'm Smurf Cat. You know. The one that says 🎵 WE LIVE WE LOVE WE LIE 🎵 "
"Oh that Smurf Cat," camera said, "you know you could have just said your name before we came inside."
"But I tried to but you inter…"
"Whatever. Nobody was stopping you to do so. Ah, but it's whatever." Camera interrupted yet again. "So, my brother is supposed to be training today so you gotta come cause I'm supposed to train… *sigh*… both of you."

Chapter 4: The Trial
"Hey!" an unexpected noise interrupted the silence, "You new here?"

"Uh… yeah I guess."
"Well I am not letting you roam these parts. Ya hear?"
"Hey," Camera called out, "Leave him alone Beluga!"
"OK. OK. But first," he started, "he has to complete the trial."
"Dun Dun… DUN" Camera said. "Sorry. Sorry."
"But it would be a very looooong walk though."

One looooong walk later:
"So… so this is th… the trial."
"Yup," Camera said casually. "If you fail only once then you would never be able to join and your whole family would be disappointed, and you will be humiliated for the REST OF YOUR LIFE! So yeah, no pressure!"
"Yeah, NO pressure." Smurf Cat said sarcastically. "So I guess I'll just… j… jump."
"WAIT!!! Don't jump. I might not be a 'meme' but… sigh… I think we could be pretty good friends."
"Otto. You shouldn't be HERE," Camera said in rage.
"Let ME do it first." Otto said.
"But…"
"I'm the best and more superior to every meme,

why thank you."

"Look, I don't know why you were even allowed <u>HERE</u>. Who let you out of your cage? How did Beluga not see you? What happened?"

"Ahhhhh…"

"Shut up, Smurf Cat!"

"Ha ha, you need therapy." Otto said.

"Yes you do and I have the perfect one."

Chapter 5: The Discussion

"This is dumb and weird," said Toothless.

"Then… why are you still listening?"

" 'cause I need to talk about the incidence."

"Oh, the incidence."

To be continued…

Untitled by Nadia

Christina fell to the floor silently. She was in a dream! Christina was dreaming about candy world. A place where beds are marshmallows and houses are gingerbread houses with sprinkles! At first, Christina questioned to herself "Where am I?"
"You are in candy world," whispered a gingerbread man. "I love this place." shouted the little girl. "It's like Alice in the world of wonder land but it's actually Alice in the world of candy land."
This was so exciting for her that she accidently broke a gingerbread house. She started eating, but after a lot of candy, cakes and all kinds of candy her tummy hurt. "Owww I have to go back home!" she said to herself. The berry powder was running out so she teleported back home. "I'm never eating a berry anymore!" she shouted.

Ukelele Magic by Olivia

Jayda picked up her favourite Golden ukelele, she played the first string. C… Kaboom SPLASH!! When she woke up she was laying on a star. "Aaaah!" screamed Jayda. "Where am I?" she asked.

Don't Do This to Your Heart by Rosalie

Don't play darts
With your heart
It will lose its spark

Spring by Lina

When I'm outside,
I can feel the cool breeze
The sun is really bright
Just like the stars
I like sitting down
And hear the birds sing
What a lovely day
I'm never going to forget again

Ocean by Olivia

As the waves wash ashore
I take my dog Roo and no one more.
The seagulls sing
And sea shells spin

Then Roo gives me her paw.

Story of The Sad Cloud by Nadia

One day many years ago, there was a cloud. She didn't have any cloud friends and she couldn't carry all the load of water.
So she fled finding a place to cry. Because she knew that crying she could unload the heavy water. Then she found a place that looked like a park. The cloud had cried with joy. So she had begun to do her job. People were happy because it hadn't rained for a long time. The tears of the cloud refreshed them. The cloud was also happy because it didn't have to carry so much weight anymore. The cloud family had come again to check if she was happy and when she saw her family, the cloud began to cry but this time with astonishment.

Charlotte and The Chandelier by Olivia

Once upon a time there was a little girl named Charlotte, and Charlotte lived in a small cottage on Matthews Rd. She has a mother who worked in a chandelier shop. One day her mum brought home a crystal clear chandelier. "My masterpiece," said mum holding it up. Ooooooh said Charlotte. No touchy! Shouted mum. Sorry about that said mum it's just that… this… chandelier… is… haunted. When it turned 9:00 Charlotte was packing a torch, a blanket and A CAGE!! This is for the ghost so when it was 9:30 she went downstairs. Mum was watching TV. Charlotte raised 3 fingers, 3 2 1 and mum was asleep.
Charlotte came down and started jumping on the sofa. Almost there and *"clink"* she touched the chandelier! Swish Swosh! A little ghost emerged from the floorboards. "Boo!" shouted the Ghost. "Aw is it Halloween already?" asked Charlotte. "You're not scared of me" said the Ghost, "um no?" said Charlotte.

Chapter 2: Pointless
"Well, sobbed the ghost, my family was right. I'm not scary!" "Oh don't go," said Charlotte.

"What's the point of staying you're not scared." "There is a point, you can help me!" "With what I'm not a genie. I don't grant wishes." "No, I know you're not a genie you're gonna need a pair of gloves though and a hammer."

"What's a hammer?" Asked the ghost. "It doesn't matter what it is it just matters that you watch your fingers." BANG CLANG BOOM!!! "Stop hitting the table, hit the chandelier." "Okay" CRAaackle CRASH the chandelier broke to pieces. "Yes yes yay," said the ghost. "I am finally free!"

Eid and Ramadan by Lina

Some of you might not know about Ramadan and Eid. It's okay, because I will tell you about it. Ramadan is when you don't eat for the whole day until 6pm! At 6pm Muslims gather together to have a big feast and pray a lot. Sometimes, people wake up at night time before 4am to eat because that's when you start fasting. I am myself a Muslim and I love it. Ramadan lasts for one month. Muslims do Ramadan to remember poor people. After that, there is a big celebration called Eid that lasts for 1 day. We give loads of presents to each other and wear traditional clothes. Muslims also wear Henna which is a special tattoo Muslims wear.

The Meaning of Life by Adelaide

Once there was a young man who always visited a park every day but was very boisterous. However, one day that all changed…
"Here he comes," said the children clearing the path like always. "Hello little ones" he chuckled patting the children's heads. "I'm still handsome and you're still pathetic." he snarled. But just then the elderly man that always did tai chi spoke. "Instead of boistering why not try tai chi?" he suggested. "I wish that thing never existed, it's for old boring people like you. I'm ashamed and embarrassed just looking at you," he said with a snort. "When your bones are sore give it a try," the elderly man said softly despite the young man's hardness. "I will never, plus my bones will never get sore. Ta ta." he said with a wave and strode off. That night in his dreams he stood unmoving in front of a gold archway. Past the gold archway a red dragon sat in a green chaise. "Who are you? Where am I"? he spluttered. "You have upset the gods of life." the dragon said. "Therefore you must be punished. Find the meaning of life and the curse will be lifted."
"You've been terribly mistaken. I'm great, everyone knows and loves me. I can't be punished, I should be awarded." he demanded. "The gods are never

wrong. You will now return to the real world." the dragon shouted furiously.

Then, he found himself back in his bed. "Just a dream," he thought with a shimmer of nervous and thankfulness in his eyes. But there was a great pain in his back. "Better fetch some pills," he thought turning to get out of bed. When he was in the kitchen he glanced at the mirror. But to his horror all he saw was an elderly man probably in his 70s or 80s.

Eventually, after three days, he decided to get some fresh air at the park. When he got there he was treated differently, everyone was smiling and saying lovely things like 'good morning.' "They've never done that before," he wondered. The old man asked if he'd do tai chi with him and the now elderly man accepted. It felt lovely stretching out his old, frail bones. "It's so warm and peaceful here," he said. "You're welcome to join me anytime." the old man said warmly. And so they both did tai chi every day from sunrise to sunset. One night in his dreams he saw the dragon again. "Well done you found the meaning of life. You will return to your old body now." the dragon said. But even so he still did tai chi with the elderly man and was more kind and thoughtful.

The Write-London Timeline

2014:
Write-London is officially founded with the advice and support of Spread the Word after Tom Mallender had been trialling and running workshops since graduating in 2010.
Work began on securing funding for our first official project, *Write-London #Hammersmith and Fulham*.

2015:
Write-London #Hammersmith and Fulham ran during early 2015. It was supported using public funding by the Arts Council England via the Grants for the Arts and the National Lottery, along with financial support from Creative Future. This was the first official Write-London project and worked with 70 participants over 11 sessions and saw us partner with: Fulham Fields, Iranian Association, Mongolian Culture Centre, Response Community Projects and St Andrew's Church.
Write London #Hammersmith and Fulham was published in 2015.

Write-London #Islington and Camden ran during the winter of 2015 and saw us work with 267 participants from the Islington and Camden community. It saw us start to work with Age UK, New Unity, and Holy Cross Centre. *Write-London #Islington and Camden* was supported using public funding by the Arts Council England via the Grants for the Arts and the National Lottery.

Write London #Islington and Camden was published in 2016.

2016 - 2017
Write-London 2016-17 ran throughout 2016 and 17 and worked with 638 participants.
The project saw two solo anthologies of work published by workshop participants:
From West Ham to Wapping to Istanbul and Back by Chris Bird and *Human Dilemmas* by Madeleine Kingston along with two collected anthologies of all participants' work: *Write-London 2016/17 Vol 1.* and *Write-London 2017 Vol 2.*

Write-London (2016) and *Write-London (2017)* were supported using public funding by the Arts

Council England via the Grants for the Arts and the National Lottery.
This project saw Write-London continue to partner with Age UK, Fulham Fields, New Unity, Response Community Projects, St Andrew's Church and also start to work with Claremont, Gospel Oak Action Link, Islington Central Library, Mind In Camden, Only Connect and Queen's Crescent Community Association.

During 2017 Write-London was a proud assist in the delivery of **Poems by Post**, a project devised and delivered by **It's Not Your Birthday But…** during which a number of Write-London participants got to engage in their first professional writing project.

When talking about Poems By Post, It's Not Your Birthday But… said:

"In 2017 we were pleased to be working with The Royal Star and Garter Homes in Surbiton.
This programme was inspired by the thought that creative outcomes may differ if stimulus was sent postally rather than electronically. Twelve residents of the home worked with lead artist Tom

Mallender to share stories and memories that were important to them. These were then used as a stimulus for poetry, which was posted to six other poets across the country from London to Newcastle, who produced work in response.
The residents were also paired with pen pals from Hinchley Wood School, who worked with artist Rachel Turner of Bounce Theatre. The older and younger pen pals shared stories and compared notes on school life, fashion, work, friends and families. The project culminated in over 35 poems being published in a dedicated anthology and the pen pals meeting at a tea party hosted by the local MP." https://itsnotyourbirthdaybut.com/poems-by-post

From September 2017 to January 2019 Write-London, Age UK Islington, London Metropolitan University and Islington Heritage Service collaborated on the **Lost Trades of Islington** project, to record the memories of those who worked in trades and industries that no longer exist in Islington today.

Age UK Islington volunteers worked with London Metropolitan University students to record the stories of 10 people who worked in these "lost trades". Write-London used these recordings for a series of poetry workshops held at the Drovers Centre and then produced a book of those poems. To celebrate the end of the project, London Metropolitan University hosted an event and exhibition as part of their Fast Forward Festival in November 2018, which included contributors talking about the industries they worked in, their working life and living in Islington, and other participants spoke about their various roles in project. The exhibition was then moved to Islington Local History Centre.

2018:
Write-London Voices from Landmarks ran during the latter half of 2018 during which time we worked with 139 participants. *Write-London Voices from Landmarks* saw Write-London work outside of London for the first time with a series of workshops delivered at Landmarks Specialist College in South Yorkshire working with young participants with learning difficulties. The smaller number of participants over previous Write-London projects was due to the focused nature of the work and the more complex needs of participants.

Alongside partnering with Landmarks Specialist College, this project saw Write-London continue to partner with Response Community Projects, Islington Central Library, Mind In Camden, Only Connect and start to work with Portugal Prints and Brent, Wandsworth & Westminster Mind. *Write-London Voices from Landmarks* saw Write-London work with the publishing specialist Holly Ainley who oversaw the creation of the Write-London anthology collecting a selection of work across all the previous Write-London projects. We were particularly proud to present work created during these sessions to a live audience of over 4,400 people through various readings and exhibitions.

Write-London Voices from Landmarks was supported using public funding by the Arts Council England via the Grants for the Arts and the National Lottery.

2019:
Write-London Unheard Voices ran during 2019 and by the end of the project we had worked with 433 participants. *Write-London Unheard Voices* saw Write-London continue to partner with Portugal

Prints, Only Connect, Islington Central Library, Mind In Camden and Brent, Wandsworth & Westminster Mind while also starting to work with the West London NHS Trust.

The *Write-London Unheard Voices* anthology was published in 2019.

Write-London Unheard Voices was supported using public funding by the Arts Council England via the Grants for the Arts and the National Lottery.

During mid-2019, Naino Masindet joined Write-London as a participant and mentee. After working on various projects, she became first an assistant facilitator, then co-facilitator before becoming well deserved co-director in 2024.

2020:
Write-London Untold Tales ran throughout 2020 and despite the challenges imposed by the pandemic, we worked with 278 participants and saw Write-London continue to partner with Portugal Prints, Brent, Wandsworth & Westminster Mind and the West London NHS Trust.

Write-London Untold Tales was published in 2020 and despite the lifting of lockdown, it was judged safest to not hold in-person events. Some work created during *Write-London Untold Tales* formed parts of exhibitions held during 2021.

Write-London Untold Tales was supported using public funding by the Arts Council England via the Grants for the Arts and the National Lottery.

From early 2020 to March 2022 Write-London was a proud assist in the delivery of **Lost Letters** a projected devised and delivered by **Is Not Your Birthday But…** .

Lost Letters was funded by The National Lottery Heritage Fund.
When talking about *Lost Letters*, It's Not Your Birthday But… said:

"Lost Letters was our flagship heritage project with Surrey History Centre to bring local history to life through creative responses to letters.

The project had been envisaged as a live experience and tour with four local partners, but Covid meant we took a different path. We provided a series of online creative challenges that anyone could freely engage with and had responses from all over the world.

We set up an online programme for residents and volunteers at the Royal Star & Garter care home to engage with Lost Letters which was well received and allowed residents to connect beyond the four rooms of their room with the support of volunteers and artists.

"Taking part in this project helped me deal with the claustrophobia of Covid and meant the four walls of my room opened up and fell away."
We delivered creative challenges as well as live and online workshops with a range of partners including The halow Project, the West London Mental Health Trust, Rocket Artists, Anstee Bridge PRU, Hinchley Wood Secondary School and 64 Million Artists." https://itsnotyourbirthdaybut.com/lost-letters

2021:
Write-London New Voices & Unheard Tales ran throughout 2021 and worked with 436 participants.

Write-London New Voices & Unheard Tales was published in 2021 and work was exhibited at four venues around the UK and saw Write-London continue to partner with West London NHS Trust, Brent, Wandsworth & Westminster Mind and Portugal Prints.

Write-London New Voices & Unheard Tales was supported using public funding by the Arts Council England via the Grants for the Arts and the National Lottery.

During 2021 we edited and published our first solo short story anthology by a Write-London writer, The *Midnight Creatures Who Tickled the Moon* by Chris Bird; a collection of short stories for young readers aged 8-12.

2022-2023:
Write-London Fresh Perspectives ran from May 2022 to September 2023 during which time we worked with 454 participants continuing our partnership with West London NHS Trust, Brent, Wandsworth & Westminster Mind and Portugal Prints.

Write-London Fresh Perspectives was supported using public funding by the Arts Council England via the Grants for the Arts and the National Lottery.

During the delivery of *Write-London Fresh Perspectives* Tom and Naino edited and published a solo volume of work by long-time Write-London participant, writer and artist Chris Bird titled "Transmissions".

Transmissions is a collection of poems, short stories and related artwork reflecting upon the author's experiences of homelessness, addiction and schizophrenia. It has been reviewed as a "must read" by several national magazines and websites.

During 2023 Write-London was exceptionally happy as part of the Hammersmith and Fulham Writers' Festival to partner with Langford Primary School, Old Oak Primary School, Sands End Arts & Community Centre (SEACC), Sands End Associated Projects In Action (SEAPIA) and Shepherds Bush Library. This collaboration saw Write-London work with almost 100 young people aged 6-12 from around the borough.

The Sands End Young People's Anthology was launched in September 2023 at Sands End Arts & Community Centre where 12 of the young people who had taken part performed their work to a packed audience of friends, family and local community members.

A second volume of work from young writers was published in February 2024 as Let's *Write Hammersmith and Fulham 2023*. The positive outcomes from this project have led to Write-London now offering a program of projects both for adults and young people.

2024:
Let's Write London ran throughout 2024 during which time we worked with 873 participants continuing our partnership with Brent, Wandsworth & Westminster Mind, Portugal Prints, Shepherds Bush Library and West London NHS Trust and to also start working with the Wellbeing & Recovery College.

Let's Write London was supported using public funding by the Arts Council England via the Grants for the Arts and the National Lottery.

As part of *Let's Write London* we were delighted to help participant Leslie Aldridge, a new writer, tell his story which we published as *A Medic's Journey to the Falklands* which was published online in November 2024 and will have a launch event alongside *Write-London: The First Ten Years* in January 2025.

During 2024 we also delivered a yearlong project for young people running a weekly after-school creative writing club hosted at SEAPIA which was officially called **Sands End Adventures in Creativity** but was quickly named "Writing Club" by the young writers themselves and we went with that name forwards. This project was funded by Dr Edwards & Bishop King's (DEBK) with some additional funding from Tideway and support from SEACC.

Sands End Adventures in Creativity was published in September 2024 to great reviews and glowing reports in the local press.

2025 onwards:

At this time of writing (December 2024) funding has been secured for a busy program of adult and young people's creative projects in 2025 which will see Write-London working in partnership with Dr Edwards & Bishop King's (DEBK), Portugal Prints, Sands End Associated Projects In Action (SEAPIA), Shepherds Bush Library, Brent, Wandsworth & Westminster Mind, Wellbeing & Recovery College, West London NHS Trust and West London Queer Project (WLQP).

We are also looking forward to hopefully working on another heritage project with It's Not Your Birthday But… .

Project Partners

Since 2014, Write-London has worked with over fifty partners on numerous projects, many of them multiple times. We would like to thank them all for making the work possible that Write-London has delivered.

Write-London: The First Ten Years contains work that has been produced in cooperation with: Age UK, Apples and Snakes, Big Ideas, Claremont, Creative Future, East Ham Library, Gospel Oak Action Link, halow Project, Hinchley Wood School, Iranian Association, Islington Central Library, Landmarks Specialist College, London Metropolitan Archives, Mind In Camden, Mongolian Culture Centre, Museum of London Docklands, New Unity, Only Connect, Queen's Crescent Community Association, Response Community Projects, Royal Star & Garter, St Andrew's, Fulham Fields, Tate Exchange, The British Museum & Young Hammersmith and Fulham Foundation.

We would like to thank the following organisations that have helped and assisted with the planning, development, administration, funding and delivery of current Write London projects and those we are working in partnership with on other projects:

Arts Council England
https://www.artscouncil.org.uk/

Write-London is supported using public funding by the Arts Council England via the Grants for the Arts and the National Lottery.

Dr Edwards & Bishop King's (DEBK)
https://www.debk.org.uk/

With a 400-year strong history of charitable giving, Dr Edwards & Bishop King's Fulham Charity (often referred to as DEBK) is a local charity that helps provide for the needs of people living in the old Metropolitan Borough of Fulham, London since 1618. Currently, our three principal grant making streams to achieve our objectives are:

• Relief in Need – We supply grants for essential items to Fulham residents on low incomes who may be referred by local welfare agencies or who may apply direct

• Grants for Organisations – We provide grants for running costs, or for projects, to organisations who are helping local people in need

• Holiday Schemes – For children who would not otherwise have a break during the school holidays

West London NHS Trust
https://www.westlondon.nhs.uk/

West London NHS Trust is an NHS trust which provides mental and physical health services to the London boroughs of Ealing, Hammersmith and Fulham and Hounslow.

Brent, Wandsworth & Westminster Mind
https://www.bwwmind.org.uk/

Brent, Wandsworth & Westminster Mind aim to deliver the best mental health services for those who live and work in the communities they serve, as well as neighbouring boroughs.

They strive to offer those with mental health problems equitable opportunities to attain the highest quality of life, addressing stigma and discrimination.

Over 50% of their staff, volunteers and trustees have their own lived experience of mental health problems helping them better understand the needs of those they are here to support.

Portugal Prints
https://www.portugalprints.co.uk/

Portugal Prints is a therapeutic arts project. We support artists living with mental health difficulties to construct a life beyond the services, a life of creativity and curiosity. We believe that art can empower people to express themselves, to learn, to build resilience and to nurture meaningful relationships.

Portugal Prints
Part of Mind in Brent, Wandsworth and Westminster

Shepherds Bush Library
https://www.lbhf.gov.uk/libraries/find-your-library/shepherds-bush-library

Located at Westfield, London, the £2 million library is one of the most exciting and innovative libraries in the country and has something for everyone. Visit the library in your lunch hour or the next time you are shopping at Westfield London! It's the place to study, surf, relax and have fun in Shepherds Bush.

h&f
hammersmith & fulham

Sands End Associated Projects In Action (SEAPIA)

https://www.seapia.org/

Everyone needs a place where they feel safe, valued and able to develop their skills.

SEAPIA provides low-cost play and childcare provisions for children aged 4-13 years, we have a purpose-built building and a large outdoor space, children are able to engage in many activities in a stimulating positive environment.

We meet the needs of our community by providing a hub where children can express themselves freely, the elderly and isolated residents can meet to share experiences and socialise with each other and the younger generation.

Surrey Poet Laureateship
https://www.surreypoetlaureateship.org/

Founded in 2024, the Surrey Poet Laureateship is dedicated to making poetry accessible, engaging, and impactful for communities across Surrey. Through initiatives like open mic nights, poetry hubs, and youth programmes, the non-profit fosters creativity, builds connections and celebrates the power of the spoken and written word. With a mission to preserve and promote Surrey's rich cultural heritage, the Laureateship provides a platform for poets of all backgrounds and experience levels to share their voices and inspire others.

It's Not Your Birthday But...
https://itsnotyourbirthdaybut.com/

It's Not Your Birthday But... (INYBB) is a not-for-profit collective of artists championing connection through creativity. We run visual arts, heritage and creative writing programmes that support people to connect, express, reflect and celebrate themselves through their own creativity. We do this in ways that are trauma-informed, person-centred, and helpful to them as experts in their own lives. We offer platforms to share their work which can positively impact both the people involved and the places they are in. We share a range of tools and techniques that enable them to build ongoing creativity into their lives.

We have a focus on creativity impacting the physical environments we work in through co-created and co-curated sharing of the work into group artworks, murals, and exhibitions. We work with people of all ages but predominantly work with young people and young adults aged 11-21 in secure settings and in alternative education provision. The majority of our work takes place in SW London and Surrey where we are based.

We run regular creative programmes at HMPYOI Feltham and Anstee Bridge, an alternative education provision for young people aged 11-16 from Kingston and Richmond. We use youth-work principles to empower young people and young adults through creativity. Our programmes focus on three core areas:

- Personal Growth
- Community Building
- Improving spaces and places through co-created art

Spread the Word
https://www.spreadtheword.org.uk

Spread the Word is London's writer development agency. They provide high quality, low cost opportunities for writers to improve their craft and develop their careers while also identifying and supporting talented writers from a diversity of backgrounds and encouraging as many people as possible to try creative writing as a means of self-expression.

Printed in Great Britain
by Amazon